Shadow Work and Healing the Inner Child

The Ultimate Guide to Integrating Your Dark Side and Restoring the Wounded Soul Within

© Copyright 2024 – All rights reserved.

The contents of this book may not be reproduced, duplicated, or transmitted without direct written permission from the author.

Under no circumstances will any legal responsibility or blame be held against the publisher for any reparation, damages, or monetary loss due to the information herein, either directly or indirectly.

Legal Notice:

This book is copyright protected. This is only for personal use. You cannot amend, distribute, sell, use, quote, or paraphrase any part or the content within this book without the consent of the author.

Disclaimer Notice:

Please note the information contained within this document is for educational and entertainment purposes only. Every attempt has been made to provide accurate, up-to-date, reliable, and complete information. No warranties of any kind are expressed or implied. Readers acknowledge that the author is not engaging in the rendering of legal, financial, medical, or professional advice. The content of this book has been derived from various sources. Please consult a licensed professional before attempting any techniques outlined in this book.

By reading this document, the reader agrees that under no circumstances is the author responsible for any losses, direct or indirect, which are incurred as a result of the use of the information contained within this document, including, but not limited to, errors, omissions, or inaccuracies.

Your Free Gift
(only available for a limited time)

Thanks for getting this book! If you want to learn more about various spirituality topics, then join Mari Silva's community and get a free guided meditation MP3 for awakening your third eye. This guided meditation mp3 is designed to open and strengthen ones third eye so you can experience a higher state of consciousness. Simply visit the link below the image to get started.

https://spiritualityspot.com/meditation

Table of Contents

PART 1: SHADOW WORK 1
   INTRODUCTION 2
   CHAPTER 1: SHADOW WORK 101 3
   CHAPTER 2: DISCOVERING AND ACCEPTING YOUR SHADOW 10
   CHAPTER 3: THE SHADOW'S MIRROR EFFECT 17
   CHAPTER 4: THE SHADOW AND AUTHENTICITY 24
   CHAPTER 5: THE SHADOW AND RELATIONSHIPS 31
   CHAPTER 6: THE SHADOW AND SOCIETY 38
   CHAPTER 7: SHADOW WORK EXERCISES 47
   CHAPTER 8: THE UPS AND DOWNS OF SHADOW WORK 56
   CHAPTER 9: BRINGING THE SHADOW INTO THE LIGHT 62
   CHAPTER 10: SHADOW WORK: A STAGE OF SPIRITUAL AWAKENING 71
   30-DAY GUIDE TO SPIRITUAL AWAKENING THROUGH SHADOW WORK 81
PART 2: HEALING THE INNER CHILD 85
   INTRODUCTION 86
   CHAPTER 1: THE INNER CHILD EXPLAINED 88
   CHAPTER 2: ARCHETYPES OF THE INNER CHILD 96
   CHAPTER 3: DISCOVERING YOUR INNER CHILD 106
   CHAPTER 4: ACCEPTING YOUR INNER CHILD 116
   CHAPTER 5: INNER CHILD MEDITATION 125
   CHAPTER 6: INNER CHILD JOURNALING 133

CHAPTER 7: INNER CHILD AWARENESS 141
CHAPTER 8: THE CHALLENGES OF HEALING YOUR INNER CHILD 149
CHAPTER 9: THE BENEFITS OF HEALING YOUR INNER CHILD 157
CHAPTER 10: HEALING YOUR INNER CHILD CHALLENGE 165
CONCLUSION 176
HERE'S ANOTHER BOOK BY MARI SILVA THAT YOU MIGHT LIKE 178
YOUR FREE GIFT (ONLY AVAILABLE FOR A LIMITED TIME) 179
REFERENCES 180

Part 1: Shadow Work

A Guide to Integrating Your Dark Side for Spiritual Awakening

Introduction

The trouble with the world today is that we're all suffering from the continued ignorance of our shadow selves. Depression, anxiety, war, and strife result from the collective shadow we all must face, starting with our personal ones. Suppose you've noticed that you've been going through harder times than usual, sabotaging yourself, ruining your prospects, relationships, and more. In that case, it might be that your shadow is asking you to pay attention to it. It's time to integrate your shadow so you can find your true, authentic self and finally heal.

Without integrating the parts of us that we've rejected, there's no chance for us to be able to connect to our souls as we're meant to. We can't find it in ourselves to grow personally, let alone spiritually. The fact that you've decided to read this book says you're aware that you need to heal yourself and look at those parts of yourself that you've rejected for a long time.

Unlike other books on this topic, this one is very easy to read, and the concepts are explained in a way anyone can grasp. Whether you're new to the process of shadow work or have been at this a while, you will find countless nuggets of gold within these pages to mine and make your life richer. Everything is written in simple English, with no esoteric concepts that might confuse the readers.

If you're ready to do the work and redeem all parts of yourself, you're in the perfect spot to do so! Keep an open mind and get ready to become whole again.

Chapter 1: Shadow Work 101

What Is the Shadow?

The shadow is a term used in metaphysics to describe the sum totality of our unconscious mind. It can be viewed as an archetype consisting of instinctual elements and emotions, representing the "dark" part of ourselves. Shadows are largely considered taboo because they are negative and uncontrollable. However, shadows are also necessary for our psychological well-being. The shadow is also described as an "other half" that exists with a person. It is considered the part of us that is not of good moral character, but others cannot see it because it is an undiscovered repressed part of ourselves. This leads to a lack of self-acceptance and confidence in one's own personality.

What Is Shadow Work?

Bring your unconscious mind to consciousness.
https://www.pexels.com/photo/adult-anger-art-black-background-356147/

The concept of shadow work refers to the process of bringing our unconscious mind into consciousness. This is done by allowing one's dark side to come out through visualization or dreams, then embracing it and not trying to hide it. With practice, the shadow will be integrated with the "light" side of ourselves and make us whole people.

Shadow work can be used as a tool in psychology and spirituality. It is used in psychology when one wishes to uncover repressed memories and can also be applied in spirituality when seeking greater knowledge of one's soul and its purpose. Among other things, shadow work is known for helping people become more aware of the things that interfere with their daily lives and what they need to do to heal themselves. This is accomplished by coming in contact with your shadow and learning how to embrace it. One seeks to understand their shadow and confront it with the light to heal the inner conflicts within themselves. Many people see the shadow as a negative thing that can only be understood when completely unearthed. However, this isn't completely accurate. After all, the shadow is also made up of some of the good things you've rejected because other people didn't accept them when you were younger.

How Is the Shadow Self Born?

Your shadow (often referred to as the "shadow self") is born when you are young, probably at a very early age. Our environment and the way we were affirmed or rejected by our parents in the first few years of our lives will play an important role in whether or not we develop a healthy sense of self. Even the shiniest of people have their dark side. This is because all humans are born with instincts, which means they will inherently wish to pursue pleasure and avoid pain. Those who cannot accept this side of themselves will develop shame as a result. These individuals usually become perfectionists and are never satisfied with their performance, no matter what.

The shadow is born from the things you reject about yourself and the bad times you experienced as a child. It consists of all the things in life that are unpleasant for us to think about, yet we suppress them and refuse to acknowledge their existence. Doing this causes us to take on destructive characteristics within ourselves to avoid dealing with the pain we have created. These characteristics can be anything from addiction problems, perfectionism, and low self-esteem.

Why You Should Meet Your Shadow

As Carl Jung said, "One does not become enlightened by imagining figures of light, but by making the darkness conscious." It is important to understand that shadows cannot be avoided. They are a part of every human being and are inescapable. Understanding this concept is an important step in learning to love yourself. As a result of your shadow work, you'll be able to acknowledge your bad side without shame and find peace with it. You'll also be able to discover and appreciate the good within you that has been hidden away for years and finally appreciate it as something worthwhile rather than rejecting it.

Jung also said, "Everyone carries a shadow, and the less it is embodied in the individual's conscious life, the blacker and denser it is." The shadow often takes on an animalistic form when we are young due to our experiences. We could be shy, quiet, introverted, or always try to be the center of attention. These characteristics are simply traits that we want others to see - not ones we wish to hide. However, those who repress their shadow prevent themselves from being able to grow into more mature and spiritually aware individuals capable of *bearing* the burdens that come with living in this world instead of being crushed by them.

When we repress the shadow, we do so because we are ashamed of it. When it was born into the world, we were small children and had no idea what a shadow was, what it meant, and why it was there. As a result, we viewed this part of ourselves as something that would cause harm to other people if they were to find out about it. This causes us to hide from our emotions, which causes us to feel isolated from the world. The repression of the shadow also makes us unable to grow to understand who we truly are, and it also makes us more susceptible to projecting our anger onto others.

How Shadow Work Leads to Spiritual Awakening

When you face your shadow, you come face to face with yourself. This is the only way we can ever have self-knowledge and a real awareness of who we are. Usually, people do not like looking at their shadows; so many have psychological problems because they're scared to know what's underneath all that clutter in their minds. It's easier for them to give in to their addictions and let the lies take over their lives and control who they think they are in society.

Shadow work involves a difficult and sometimes painful process of bringing your unconscious into the light of consciousness. It allows you to come to a point where you discover your repressed inner aspects. Your shadow is not something to be feared but rather a part of you that needs to be understood and embraced as your nature. Your conscious mind also needs to know how to work with it for you to reach spiritual awakening. Unfortunately, many people do not understand that their psyche or unconscious mind has a purpose and function and often reject this momentous fact.

How Does Shadow Work, Work?

Shadow work is a long process of conscious discovery during which you confront your repressed personality traits (personalities and behavior patterns) and become the practitioner of the Self. It is this self-knowledge that leads to personal enlightenment and spiritual awakening. During shadow work, one learns to see oneself as part of the inner and outer world. When we can perceive ourselves fully, we transcend the boundaries between inner and outer experience.

In Jungian psychology, shadow work entails the visual mental imagery necessary for dealing with unconscious psychological issues such as aggression. One must learn how to deal with and visualize the shadow rather than allowing it to consume one's life. Many people who undergo shadow work find it difficult and frustrating. Although many of us want to deny our true personality, there is no getting around the fact that *we are who we are*. You don't have to change your shadow – you simply have to accept it for what it is. Once you can do this, your shadow will no longer take control over the direction of your life, and it will cease being a hindrance in your spiritual awakening process.

Carl Jung was aware of the key importance of the shadow. He wrote about the necessity of understanding how one's shadow is necessary for growth and maturity. He even made explicit statements about why one needs to work on their shadow side to be free of its negative influences and destructive behaviors. Jung considered this aspect to be a vital step toward self-knowledge and personal enlightenment. Though we are all marked by our shadow, we can learn to reconcile it with the rest of who we are.

Myths about Shadow Work

Let's address some of the common myths and misconceptions surrounding the concepts of shadow work and the shadow itself.

1. **You're a bad person for having a shadow**: The shadow isn't inherently evil. It is a part of you that was never explored – it only became associated with negative emotions based on external social archetypes.
2. **You're alone in wanting to work on your shadow:** Many people want to work through their shadows and spiritual awakenings. In fact, it's a large community of people who are interested in the same topics and have been struggling with the same issues you have.
3. **You're weak if you don't want to deal with your shadow:** Many people avoid working through their shadows until they feel ready. Waiting doesn't make you weak or a coward; the fact is, none of us knows when we will be ready to deal with our emotional issues. Sometimes we can go through a dark period lasting many years without ever confronting it. When it's time, you'll know it.
4. **Your shadow isn't important:** Your shadow is an integral part of who you are and why you are the way you are today. It needs to be understood if you want to break the bonds of your past and begin a new phase of spiritual awakening. You're wrong if you think you can get rid of it and not have any consequences.
5. **Shadow work is impossible and pointless:** No, it doesn't have to be either. There is nothing to be afraid of, and there are plenty of reasons why shadow work can be worthwhile. It can help you cope with the emotions of your past and give you a better understanding of yourself and your identity. If you've been self-sabotaging yourself and can't figure out why perhaps it's time to say hello to the darkness.

How the Shadow Self Sabotages

Your shadow self can keep you from making money: Your shadow can be a major obstacle behind your lack of financial gain. Since your shadow is a side of yourself that you have repressed and labeled negative, it tends to have a dark and destructive view of money. You may be unable to see anything positive about money because you subconsciously fear it (or were never taught this positive perspective). If you are consistently making sub-par money, it could be because your shadow self is leading you into situations that will make more sense to you to deal with your emotions. It could also be that your true talents, which would bring you success, are buried in the shadow and need to be brought to light to do well.

Your shadow sabotages love relationships: One of the ways in which your shadow can cause problems in love relationships is by undermining what's good about them. It always seeks to keep you from being happy. If you work through your shadow, it will change its ways and let you healthily experience love. Many things can keep your shadow from allowing the good things in your relationship to blossom. Perhaps a part of you desires to remain single and isolated (the loner archetype), or you want something more than what is available (the envious archetype). Perhaps also, you're unable to love because of the fear of rejection (an aspect of yourself that puts up emotional walls when others get too close), which could also be why you attract the wrong partners.

Your shadow can prevent you from having a healthy body: Your shadow self could also be behind your body's lack of health. Perhaps you're unaware of your sensitivity to certain foods or not getting enough sun and exercise. It could also be that your need for control leads you to do too much for yourself instead of doing the things which will make your body happy (like treating it with some delicious food). You might even be unable to lose weight because your shadow aspect feels unsafe and views fat as a protective mechanism.

Your shadow can keep you from enjoying life: Your shadow self could be the problem behind your inability to enjoy life. Perhaps there is too much anxiety and fear in your life – or you are always trying to control everything around you instead of allowing yourself to live spontaneously and enjoy the moment. Working on your shadow can also help increase the happiness in your life. It can show you how to work through your past emotions and let go of them so you can enjoy new experiences. It will also teach you how to accept yourself for who you are and stop getting mad at yourself when things aren't going your way.

Your shadow makes it hard for people to love you: Your shadow can make it difficult for others to see the good things about you. Maybe you're the sort of person who cannot see the good in yourself, talk down on yourself and act out so much that you convince others that you truly aren't worthy of their love. Then they will be more likely to dismiss or abandon you or make your relationships more difficult. You may even attract people who don't care about your needs, and it will take them longer to come around once they've gotten to know you better.

Quiz: How Dominant Is Your Shadow?

1. I believe that something is wrong with me that requires me to constantly control everything around me.
2. I feel like nothing I do is good enough, no matter how much I achieve or what others say about it.
3. My need to be in control of everything around me prevents anyone from getting too close to me and hurts my relationships.
4. I have trouble seeing the good in myself, and I overreact every time someone has a compliment to give.
5. My mood depends on what is going on around me and how things are going. If people start making a fuss, it will be hard for me to remain happy.
6. I feel unhappy with myself even though it doesn't seem that way to everyone.
7. My projects sometimes go bad, and it seems like things are crumbling apart around me, despite my best efforts.
8. Everything around me seems to fall apart because I am too attached, and my emotions are getting in the way of my best efforts.
9. I find myself suddenly and inexplicably overcome with negative emotions.
10. I somehow manage to do or say just the perfect thing to ruin my chances at success.

If you answered yes to six or more of these questions, your shadow is likely dominant and asks that you address it now.

Chapter 2: Discovering and Accepting Your Shadow

Before we talk about what is required for you to discover your shadow (let alone get comfortable enough to accept it), we need to define the keywords "discovery" and "acceptance." The discovery process is about finding something that has always been wherever it is. It's about disclosing the location or whereabouts of whatever you seek. The point to note here is that sometimes you cannot find what you're looking for, and this is why many people do not even know that they have a shadow aspect. In fact, you might be able to think of someone right now who you could never envision having a shadow side. For instance, the thought that Mother Theresa would have a darker aspect is something many cannot fathom.

Acceptance means coming to terms with the existence or truth of something. It's about the process of learning what the thing is and knowing that it is valid as it is, rather than seeking to get rid of or fight it. Upon learning that we all have a shadow, some people seek to abolish it, but that's not how it works. You want to integrate the shadow with the light because it is a part of you. If you reject a part of yourself, you only render yourself more helpless to the shadow. In fact, it is because of rejection that your shadow self came to exist in the first place.

What It Means to Discover and Accept Your Shadow

You might have difficulty believing that you have a shadow side, but think of it this way. Everyone has something dark in them. Maybe you're prone to being unnecessarily mean sometimes or taking pleasure in the misfortune of others. Or, maybe the more insecure part of you wants everyone around you to be exactly as miserable and self-doubting as you so that they validate your feelings with their actions. The point is that everyone has some kind of dark aspect, but it's not necessarily because they are terrible people. It's more about their shadow side being constantly there but kept under wraps until they feel the need to rise and reveal themselves. When your shadow comes out and goes active, you may or may not be in a "bad" mood. You might be in a pessimistic or anxious state, but the person inside – who has repressed it for so long – could be far worse than you realize.

Many people fear their shadow side so much that they go on living as if it isn't even there. This can sometimes be a kind of coping mechanism but also a way of denying your true self or your shadow self. This is why it's essential to discover and accept your shadow. It's the best way to accomplish spiritual well-being and awakening.

What Is Spiritual Awakening, and How Is It Connected to the Shadow Self?

Spiritual awakening is a broad term that refers to the experience you undergo as you move from being unconscious and unaware to more conscious and aware. This includes having control over your life situations, thoughts, and emotions. It's about awakening to the meaning of life. To get a clearer idea of what this means, let's analyze that thought process through the lens of Carl Jung.

Carl Jung believed that to become more conscious and aware, we must confront our shadow parts and make peace with them. To do this, we must release the repressed and twisted inside us. We must let go of the pain and suffering that a misguided identity or ego can cause. We must also accept ourselves and realize that we are all human beings who make mistakes. At the same time, we must recognize our potential for greatness and do what it takes to get there.

All of this is connected to a concept called individuation. It basically refers to your identity or ego becoming individualized, so you are no longer like everyone else but instead shaped by your perspective & experiences in life thus far. Individuation is one of the most important concepts in psychology, especially because it applies so strongly to your shadow self. Embracing your unconscious thinking and emotions and learning to work with them for good leads to individuation, which allows you to awaken spiritually.

Why You Must Accept Your Flaws to Progress Spiritually

Accepting your flaws takes away the power they have over you: One of the ways you can start waking up to your shadow self is by accepting it. This means you stop struggling against it or try hiding it from others. Instead, you realize that the shadow self is okay and part of who you are. Admitting that we have these flawed perspectives and beliefs can be very dark and painful at times, but as long as we don't reject them, they won't control us and make us sick or unhappy.

Accepting your flaws will help you grow: Another way accepting your flaws helps you is by making you more aware of things. If you're constantly fighting and escaping your shadow self, it's hard to be aware and see that things in this world can help shape who you become. However, accepting everything about who you are and what makes up your personality gives you a greater perspective. Plus, we all have our share of flaws. Rather than being ashamed of these human characteristics, embrace them and do something about them.

Accepting your flaws will allow you to become more like yourself: When you accept your flaws, you start realizing that you're not who you thought you were. For example, say that someone believed they were a kind and loving person, but then they discover their dark side that wants to hurt people. This can be very confusing and scary for them because they were raised to believe that bad things will happen to them if they behave badly. However, suppose they stop fighting against themselves and learn to accept who they are inside and what their shadow self has taught them throughout their lives. In that case, it's easier to see the truth about themselves. When one confronts the truth about themselves, they can effectively work to improve.

Accepting both the light and dark sides of yourself will help you be more objective: By accepting everything about who we are and what shapes our personalities, we stop projecting our flaws onto other people. For example, if you struggle with negative thoughts, you may project these thoughts onto the people around you. Instead of taking responsibility for them, it's easier to blame them. This very common pattern leads to fighting, arguments, and strife that can destroy relationships.

Signs of Discovering and Accepting the Shadow

Let's look at six signs that indicate you're on track to finding and accepting your shadow.

1. **What other people do no longer triggers you like it used to:** When you start accepting your shadow self, it almost feels like the world has become safer and more *right*. That's because, now that you've accepted who you are, what other people do is no longer a trigger for you. This means that being upset with people for doing something is just a misunderstanding and not about who these people are to you.
2. **You no longer engage in denial or blaming others:** This is a key sign you're getting close to discovering and accepting your shadow. You no longer deny who you are or what these negative thoughts tell you. You realize that there's nothing wrong with yourself and your subconscious; those thoughts are just a projection of how you feel deep down inside. You stop blaming others for your struggles and no longer blame yourself.
3. **You no longer get upset or angry when you see others with dark sides:** You realize that all human beings have good and bad sides. These character traits may come out at different times in a person's life; who they are today results from their earlier experiences, and you know that they were raised by flawed parents or in a less-than-perfect environment.
4. **You're no longer afraid to be seen or heard:** Once you've accepted your shadow self, you gain the courage to come out of hiding. This means that you no longer fear the light because you realize *it can't hurt you*. After all, the light and dark parts of yourself make up who you are and what makes up your personality. This is another

big step in healing because it allows you to do what feels comfortable without living a lie anymore.

5. **You no longer feel alone or isolated:** It's common for people with a shadow self to feel disconnected from others because they have trouble accepting their flaws and being seen in public. However, once they accept them, they see that there's nothing wrong with them and start enjoying the company of others again.

Side Effects of Shadow Work

You start to notice how you've deceived yourself.

When doing shadow work, you will likely suddenly notice how your mind has distorted the way you perceive the world around you – and how you perceive yourself. You'll find that some of your perceptions couldn't be further from the truth. You will also be easier on people who haven't gotten to the point of being able to see their self-deceit either.

Tip: At first, it can be rather problematic when you discover how much you've been blind to, but the key to working through that confusion is to be gentle with yourself. Don't allow yourself to wallow in self-hate or self-pity.

You realize just how much you've struggled to control things – and that you no longer need to do that.

You may have done your best to rein yourself in because you don't want to act out or may have tried to control others around you to create your "ideal" version of how life should be. When you're doing shadow work, you'll start to realize the futility of trying to make everything perfect. You will naturally relinquish your need to be in charge of everything all the time, which can be incredibly freeing.

Tip: In the beginning, it's going to be pretty scary. This is because you've gone your entire life making sure there are no unknowns and that you're always ready even for the most unlikely events and scenarios. Learn to think of this as a rollercoaster. You're on the ride; you can't get off until it's over, so you might as well turn those screams of terror into excitement and roll with the process.

You develop a form of tunnel vision when it comes to your creativity.

Accepting your shadow means that you'll be able to easily connect with your creative side, to the exclusion of everything else and without getting distracted. You'll be able to marry different concepts together in a way that works for one and all. The trouble is that some people don't know how to ground their creativity in realism because it's all-new for them, which could lead them to make detrimental decisions, especially in their relationships.

Tip: Enjoy your newfound creativity, but always take a moment to absorb what's really happening in the world around you so that you don't miss the important things and get lost in a never-ending stream of ideas.

You might seem a little cold and standoffish to other people.

As you get more involved in shadow work, you'll find that you're more aware of what others choose to do and say, and you can see through all that right to the heart of their motives. Your ability to see through the heart of a "despicable" person like a serial killer, for instance, will lead to you having a different take on things than most people. In other words, it's not that you'd justify their behavior, but you might be able to see how past trauma and wounds could have led them to become who they were. People might misrepresent your idea as defending evil, but you're not. You're simply more aware of their motivations and more compassionate than others.

Tip: Always strive for mutual understanding in your communications with others, and you shouldn't have a problem connecting with those who matter. Also, it will be clear to those who get it that you're anything but standoffish.

You no longer care for customary ways of doing things.

The thing about our culture and what we hold dear in society is that society itself also has its own shadows. When society deems a thing good or bad, you can rest assured that while people try to be good, their shadows will have the "bad" in them. Those aware of their shadows no longer allow themselves to feel shame about their "wrong" behaviors, choosing to forgive themselves. They know that these desires are in us all, and so they don't care whether or not the world and its traditions deem them to be a terrible person. For instance, maybe in the past, you were a Christian who truly believed it was bad to be rich, but you've now realized that while your desire to be rich would be frowned upon by some Christians, you no longer care for those restrictions; they no longer define you. You can live your life as your authentic self.

Tip: Try to be patient with others. Not everyone is aware of the unnecessary restrictions inherent in tradition and culture, and some people need those structures to have some sense of purpose and stability in their lives. Don't judge them for it.

Things You Can Do to Discover Your Shadow

1. **Look inwards:** Find a quiet place where you can sit alone and listen to what your subconscious says. If you're scared or nervous, acknowledge those feelings and then continue listening to what your inner self says.
2. **Face the things that scare you:** Whatever the monster in the closet is for you, decide that you'll stop running and start facing your fears. By doing this repeatedly, you realize there's nothing to be afraid of because everything inside of you is normal and okay.
3. **Accept yourself:** Decide that it's okay to accept who you are even if - sometimes -you don't like some things about yourself.
4. **Stop fighting against yourself:** Once you've accepted who you are, stop fighting against your shadow side. In other words, give up the battle that you're not going to be negative anymore. Instead, start looking at negative feelings as a normal part of who you are and what makes up your personality.

Quiz: Have You Truly Discovered and Accepted Your Shadow?

1. Have you accepted who your true self is?
2. Can you accept the negative aspects of your personality by looking at them as a normal part of who you are and what makes up "you"?
3. Do you accept who others are - even if what they *do* bothers or hurts you?
4. Do you find it easier to process your negative emotions and not judge others?
5. Have you stopped blaming others for anxiety, anger, fear, sadness, trouble with social situations, etc.?

If you answered yes to three out of five questions, it means you're making progress with your shadow work; keep working at it!

Chapter 3: The Shadow's Mirror Effect

Mirrors are very important when it comes to spirituality, discovering who you are, and exactly *what it is* you need to heal. Regarding cognitive psychology, many studies have centered on working with mirrors to come to terms with self-consciousness and self-identity. Also, you don't need to think about the mirror effect in terms of working with an actual mirror alone and seeing what the world mirrors back to you. Your experience of the world is just a reflection of who you are. This is a tough bit of truth to chew on, but when you really consider it, you'll see why it's important to change yourself first if you want the world around you to change.

Let's give a little more thought to the concept of mirroring. The mirror will copy what you're observing perfectly and right away. Also, it doesn't have any actual imperfections in how it reflects back to you. They will copy your expressions and can affect you emotionally on an unconscious level. For instance, watching yourself smile in the mirror will naturally induce feelings of happiness within you.

Mirror Work

The mirror effect allows you to see the truth of your soul.
https://www.pexels.com/photo/photo-of-man-looking-at-the-mirror-1134184/

Mirror work is a simple thing that will change your life and help you integrate all aspects of your shadow, including your wounds. This will help you learn to truly love yourself. Rooted in the philosophies of Carl Jung, the mirror work technique was created by Louise Hay to help people learn to love themselves. It's supposed to help you change how you relate with yourself to effectively change how you relate with others and your world. It's meant to teach you to love and care for yourself fully.

If you stare in the mirror for just five minutes, maintaining eye contact with yourself and being gentle about it, you might notice some interesting emotions welling up within you. You may start to feel awkward or a bit embarrassed, and you may even begin to judge and loathe yourself. The question is, why does this happen?

According to Louise Hay, the mirror will always show you what you feel about yourself. It lets you know what holds you back from full self-love and where you're doing just fine. It can also reveal to you the thoughts you've to get rid of or implement to feel more fulfilled. Andy Fox said, "In our own mirror, we can see the soul's truth." You can't hide from the truth, and you'll gain a level of intimacy with it that may leave you feeling uneasy if you don't learn how to silence your inner critic. Things you didn't even know you thought about yourself come to the surface of the conscious mind.

The Pros of Mirror Work with Shadow Work

To be clear, both of these things can be very uncomfortable at first, but when you stick with the process, you'll find incredible healing. These are some of the most powerful processes of ascending spiritually. You won't have to spend money to make this happen or sequester yourself away from life. Mirror work is something you can easily incorporate into your daily life. You only need a mirror, an open mind, and the ability to remain present all through the process. Here's why you should consider doing mirror work:

It's a form of self-love: You'll learn to truly love yourself through mirror work. This is a process that will help you to reflect on your inner light and embrace it fully. It can be quite hard to feel this way when your self-image has been wounded, but you will have no problem healing yourself with such a simple process. You'll learn how to love the person staring back at you in the mirror by accepting yourself for everything that makes up who you are. This isn't easy to do, as your wounds from the past can make it difficult for you to accept and love yourself.

You're forced to face the parts of you that you're not proud of: You'll learn to face and love the parts of your past that you're not proud of and come to grips with who you are and what it is about yourself that makes you who you are today. You'll admit to your mistakes, even those that spurn regrets and make you feel horrible. It's all part of the healing process. You can also actively choose to forgive yourself through this process because forgiveness is a part of healing.

You learn how to be vulnerable: You'll learn how to accept your vulnerabilities and embrace them as a natural part of being alive and a way to help protect yourself from further harm. You can't change your past and the fact that you've made mistakes. You'll need to work through it to learn how to accept yourself.

You learn to stop judging: One of the most powerful parts of mirror work is that you'll learn how to let go of all the judgments and criticisms you have about yourself. This will help open up your mind and heart so that they're more receptive to healing and more open when it comes to loving yourself and others. When your mind is free from these judgments, you won't feel trapped in a prison of negativity and pain. Instead, you will feel like an open book, ready to receive all the healing you need.

You learn to accept others: When your mind is free from judgments, you can truly make the shift from seeing others as a reflection of your own shadow and how they're hurting or bothering you to seeing them for who they are and the way they feel about themselves. You'll begin to accept others for their gifts and learn to love them on their own terms. Rather than being so caught up in how you think things should be or what other people should be doing, it prevents you from loving yourself and caring about what's going on in your life.

Guide to Mirror Work

1. **Commit to this:** When it comes to mirror work, you have to first decide you're going to see it through. It's a good idea to dedicate about two to five minutes each day at the very least. Ideally, it's best to go for ten minutes per session.
2. **Consider the best time of day to do this work:** You're not going to get better results picking one time of day over another. Most people get into mirror work either first thing when they wake up or the last thing before going to bed. If you like, you can just do it each time you pass by a mirror. If you don't have access to a mirror, you can use your phone camera's selfie option. You're also going to need some privacy, so keep that in mind.
3. **Pick your affirmations:** You can create your own affirmations if you like and work with them because you'll need them to counteract the negative thoughts that will arise as you gently gaze into your eyes in the mirror. These words will help you reprogram your mind to think better of yourself. You could work with many already scripted affirmations, but in my experience, it's much better to spontaneously allow them to flow in response to whatever you're feeling. For instance, if you notice a feeling of discomfort while sitting in front of the mirror, you can affirm to yourself, "I have a lovely heart and soul," or "I am comfortable with myself, and I accept myself the way I am." At the end of this guide, you will find affirmations you can work with to help you.
4. **Say your affirmation repeatedly, feeling each word:** You should say each affirmation you've chosen to work with at least ten times. You can say them in your mind or out loud. Don't go for 100 repetitions like others recommend because you don't want to turn this into a boring chore and get to the point where the words lose

meaning and feeling. Make sure to really ponder what each word means to you, as this is what will create the change you seek. Make sure you're staring yourself right in the eyes as you affirm the words. You can also address yourself using your name, which will drive the message deeper and faster into your unconscious mind.

5. **Welcome the emotions that come up:** As you do this work, you'll feel all sorts of things. Whatever it is that comes up, allow yourself to feel it. It's okay to laugh, cry, or react in any way that feels natural to you. It's good practice to hug yourself as well. It may sound silly, but you're really going to feel it. Some of the things you feel will come from your childhood can be really intense. If that happens, you need to be ready to accept your inner, wounded child as they are. Use reassuring words with them. Let them know you're here for them, love them, and understand them.

6. **Feel your heart:** Keep your hand over it as you do the work. You may feel drawn to rub that area in a circle or pat it gently or firmly. Just give in to the moment and whatever it is you need. If you feel you're too overwhelmed from doing that, it's okay to take a break and return to the process later. However, the odds are that whatever comes up at the moment is *exactly* what you need to feel and is just right; don't let your emotions and thoughts frighten you. The hand over your heart will help you connect with your body and your true self and put you in touch with the vibration of love.

7. **Write down what you discover**: You'll need a journal to refer to as you do your mirror work. This is because you're going to get insight into your shadow self as you do the work and learn what you need to do and change to bring your shadow self into the rest of you so that you're a fully integrated person. When you write down your insights, you'll have something to reflect on to show you how to live a more fulfilled life. Your journal doesn't need to be organized, and you don't have to write a full book on each session. Just note what you feel and think and the sensations that arose during your session. You don't have to make an entry in your journal every day after the session, but it's worth having one for when you get new, profound insights into your life. It's handy for seeing just how far you've come.

Spot Your Shadow in Action

The thing about the shadow is that it's *not so easy to spot*. It's the part of you that can be really elusive unless – or until – it sabotages your life enough that you have no choice but to pause and ask yourself why nothing works out, despite your best intentions. Here are a few things you can do to catch your shadow in action.

1. **Notice when you make judgments about people.** When you judge others, believe it or not, you're really judging yourself. The reason is that the things that trigger you about other people are the same things that you can consciously or subconsciously recognize in yourself. Your judgments are actually rooted in the weaknesses you perceive. This weakness is what you were taught as a young one and throughout your adult life to suppress and reject, causing it to become part of your shadow. Another thing to note about judgment is that we only ever judge those who we feel we're better than, those we think we can "lord it over." Yet the funny thing is that the judgments we make say more about us and what makes us insecure than the object of our disdain.

2. **Notice when you project your problems onto other people.** Shadow projection is very real. We get involved in a process to defend ourselves from dealing with our issues. Instead of owning them, part of the rejection process is us casting all the emotions and thoughts we have about ourselves that we don't want to deal with onto someone else. When you don't like a certain thing about yourself, you tend to see it in others whether or not it's there. The more you project your issues onto others, the more you feed your shadow. For instance, you could think of someone as too full of themselves when you're actually an arrogant person. How else would you be able to recognize that attribute in them, real or perceived? This is why those who cheat on their partners or lie to them will accuse their loved ones of doing the same thing. People who don't like their bodies laugh at others for how they look.

3. **Pay attention to your triggers.** When something causes you to have an intense emotional reaction, you should stop and ask yourself why. In being introspective like this, you'll likely see that your shadow is poking its head into the window of your life to say hello. Triggers are often what we have as a result of some event that was traumatic to us that we may have "forgotten" through repression.

They're basically your Achilles' heel. When you can take the time to understand your triggers, you'll learn more about your shadow.

4. **Notice your tendency to hurt people when you feel there are no consequences.** For instance, let's assume you engage in trolling others to hurt them online. You're fully aware it's not the right thing to do, yet you do it anyway. Why is that? Your shadow makes itself known in times when there's no consequence to face for your actions and words. You're unafraid to show the very worst aspects of yourself because, as far as you're concerned, "No one would ever know." So, notice how you deal with things when there's no one around. Even if you're the one person who likes to help the old lady with the grocery bag across the street, pause to ask yourself if this is something you would do if no one were around to notice how nice you are.

5. **Notice how you treat those you're in charge of.** For instance, you could have a terrible time at home, or your boss may have torn you a new one for something. Maybe you perceive in both situations that there's nothing you could do to your lover or your boss, so instead, you take out your frustrations on those who you have authority over. For instance, you could have angry outbursts that aren't justified on those you manage – including your kids. You could even be on the lookout for that one stranger who'll cross your path so that you can let them have it instead.

6. **Pay attention to your penchant for playing the victim card.** If you consider yourself the victim, you always have that "woe is me" attitude going on, wallowing in self-pity. When things go wrong, rather than looking for your part in the problem or considering how to move forward, you'd blame other people. Responsibility is just not your thing. Also, you likely have trouble trusting people because people are the issue as far as you're concerned. You come off as helpless and weak, even though, in an insidious way, that's a method of control as you make others do your bidding out of false obligation and guilt. You have no limits, which in addition to your low confidence, makes you very susceptible to being taken advantage of by the people in your life. You have a "me against the world" attitude, and you're always spoiling for a fight. Those who continue to play victim tend to be miserable because of it, which fuels issues like depression and anxiety. If this sounds like you, know that victimhood is one of the ways the shadow presents itself.

Chapter 4: The Shadow and Authenticity

Authenticity is about being who you really are. We live in a world where daring to be yourself is considered enough to "cancel" you and deem you unfit to be part of a group. In part, we can thank social media – where everyone wants to be relevant and follow the crowd irrespective of one's own perspective. People who have different opinions are being silenced by bullying. Those who don't have enough courage to maintain their difference of opinion feel the pressure to go along with the mob because they've seen what happens when you start singing a slightly different tune.

As a result, it's hard to find authentic people in this day and age. Instead, many of us suppress our truths and the aspects of us that we feel our tribe will not agree with. This, of course, causes the shadow self to grow stronger each day. In the real sense, authenticity is being who you are, regardless of whether anyone is on your side or not. It's daring to be yourself, present your truths as you see them, and remain un-swayed by the threats of being excommunicated from some group or "canceled" on the internet. This, of course, is not an easy thing to do. It can be a constant struggle to not feel the need to curate the best parts of myself from one situation to the next; we struggle with this daily – some more consciously than others.

Inauthenticity, the Shadow, and Spiritual Growth

When you're not true to who you are, you're repressing the aspects that you consider undesirable, which will naturally cause your shadow to grow stronger. It is virtually impossible to grow personally and spiritually if we do not stay true to ourselves. As Carl Jung puts it, "That which you most need will be found where you least want to look." If you've felt like you're stuck in a rut lately, it might be good to consider looking at how authentic you've been lately.

To grow spiritually, you're going to have to live authentically. This means following the urges that your soul lays within your heart. But each time you seek to pursue it only to allow yourself to be silenced for whatever reason, you keep yourself from spiritual growth and expansion.

You must develop the courage to face yourself, your shadow, and your inauthentic behavior. The longer you put it off, the more damage you'll do to yourself, your relationships, and your life. On this inner journey of self-discovery and authenticity, many people experience the depths of despair, which is natural. It's crucial to remember that you need this darkness to see the light.

Becoming conscious of our compulsive patterns (and shedding light on those unconscious ones) will help unify both parts of our psyches. There are many ways to interpret this spiritual growth process in practice, but one thing's for sure: it requires a willingness to face your shadow. Anything less than that will lead to stagnation and isolation.

We need the opportunity to grow to come closer to knowing ourselves, which is why it is important to see our wrongdoings and learn from them. In some cases, that's all we need to release ourselves from a self-loathing perspective. We must become aware of our unconscious, embrace it at times, and know that it is an essential part of who we are.

When you feel stuck, try bringing the shadow into your consciousness by simply observing yourself from a space outside yourself. Try not to attach judgment or criticism to any aspect of yourself (or others), but instead understand that this feeling is rooted within you and is part of how you deal with things. There's no need to blame any person or the circumstances; just observe whatever thoughts come up and keep holding still.

Repression Breeds Regression

One of the best ways to identify something that you're repressing is to look for patterns and behaviors that you create in your life by holding back from these parts of yourself. It's important to understand that the more we repress, the easier it is for us to do so. This, in turn, makes us more susceptible to wild conspiracy theories, where we label people as "bad" and fixate on them obsessively. It's often easy to understand why people feel this way if they have a negative history with certain aspects of their personality.

How can you find peace within if you're repressing a part of yourself? You'll only take many steps backward, spiritually speaking. When fear and judgment exist, we also repress the truth about ourselves because fear keeps us locked in a cycle of continuous suppression of our shadow. When we stop running and hiding from these parts of ourselves and embrace them instead, it goes a long way toward confronting the fears that arise in our lives. This can have great benefits for those who are open to it.

The shadow is not just something that affects or influences us internally; it also affects our external *reality*. You see this in certain political situations where people take on the characteristics of the very person they chose to vilify.

When we repress our shadow, we give it power over us, letting it know we won't fight back and that we'll allow ourselves to be ruled by some part or aspects of ourselves. Or, in some cases, people will hold a grudge against another person and let their mood or emotional state control them because they want to get back at them for one reason or another.

Confronting your shadow is one of the biggest challenges you'll ever face; you'll need the courage to do that. Accept that the shadow lurks within the recesses of the unconscious and that it is largely made up of repressed instinctual drives.

Put Up Your Dukes and Fight for What You Want

When we don't stay true to ourselves, it's easy to get caught up in a cycle of self-loathing where we feel trapped in our bodies and minds. We will often judge ourselves harshly while also judging others. The first step is always to observe yourself without attaching any judgment or criticism to what you find – simply observe it without judgment.

We need to observe these patterns and behaviors in our lives and how they affect us. Let yourself get as much information as you can about these "dark" parts of yourself, then let them go with love. This is how you become authentic and allow yourself to awaken spiritually.

Some people learn to ignore or mask the shadow, while others act it out negatively. You'll find that some people are more affected by their shadow than others, but all of us are affected by our selfishness at times. It's normal – it's just part of being human – but not something we have to let rule over us.

To awaken from this shadow self and become authentic, we must shed light on our unconscious, compulsive behavior. The more we struggle, the stronger it will hold onto us. The more we let go of it, the less of an effect it will have on us. You'll learn to accept that you have a shadow part of yourself – just like everyone else.

A Guide to Identifying Your Authentic Self

Identifying your authentic self is a very personal process and requires a willingness to explore yourself. It's not about being perfect; it's about being real with yourself and learning to accept that part of yourself that you don't really like.

When you're young, you often don't have the necessary tools to uncover your shadow or get to know your authentic self. This is why staying connected with your inner child as much as possible is important. Your child is always waiting for you as it understands that nobody loves them unconditionally as they do. They crave acceptance and understanding from their caregivers, even when they don't necessarily deserve it.

It's important to be patient with yourself as you go through this process. The more you are willing to take the time to self-reflect, the greater chances you have of uncovering some things that will make you a happier person.

There are a few things that will help in identifying your authentic self:
1. **Begin taking personal inventory:** First, check in with yourself to know when you feel most honest and authentic. You'll have to be courageous as you ask yourself questions and tell yourself the truth. Truth is important because the last thing you want is more

repression by hiding behind a mask or embodying values that aren't true to who you are. When you're clear on what matters to you, it will be easier to take action and make decisions. So, ask yourself, where do you feel most alive? Who do you love to hang out with the most; who brings out the best in you? What sorts of activities do you love to engage in? What aspects of your life are you most unhappy or upset about? What is it that you *know is* toxic and needs to go?

From there, you can go even deeper with this. For instance, whenever you're in a situation that doesn't feel good to you, take a second to figure out what's going on. Who's with you when you feel less than good? What are the emotions coursing through you, and what is the price you have to pay when these negative situations happen? Do the same for situations where you feel your best and most authentic self. This will help you see what you've got to change.

2. **Ground yourself in the present moment:** Figure out what's happening in the *here and now*. The less attention you pay to the past, the more room there is to make proper decisions in the future. The more you relax and go with the flow, the easier it will be to act authentically. To do this well, you shouldn't be focused on thinking about things that have already happened. When something triggers an emotion or a feeling inside you, let it be there until it dies down on its own. Then take a few minutes, or as long as it takes, to figure out how you feel about what's happening at this moment and how your past experiences affected your current feelings.

3. **Create a support system you can lean on:** One of the most important things you can do is create relationships that ground you and support you in being your authentic self. Surround yourself with people who are committed to your success and help you move forward positively. Find people who will understand your struggles, doubts, and fears; they can help when things get difficult. As long as they're also committed to personal growth, they'll have enough integrity that they won't exploit your weaknesses - or your ability to be vulnerable. Having a strong support system is one of the most important parts of personal transformation because it helps minimize the stress from within so you can focus on what's happening in the present moment.

4. **Always speak the truth with love and assertion:** Don't be afraid to speak up for yourself. You want to express what you truly want and how you truly feel about something. It will likely be a challenge and can even result in unhappiness if you don't do so from a place of love and care for yourself. As long as it's coming from your heart, other people will always respect this truth that hasn't been watered down by compromise or a lack of assertiveness.
5. **Don't dwell on what others think:** Another way to ensure that your authentic self comes through is never taking things personally when others act negatively toward you or criticize your actions or choices. What matters is how they treat those who they love and care about. When you see the world through this lens, you see that people's actions are always determined by how they feel about themselves and their perceptions of others. These are *their issues*, not yours. This doesn't mean you need to tolerate abusive behavior from others, but you can avoid pain if you focus on yourself and how other people treat important people in their lives.
6. **Try being authentic with another person:** Experiment with being your authentic self with another person or even several people. You'll most likely be surprised about how well this works out as long as you're willing to take a risk and put yourself out there. It will sometimes be uncomfortable, but it will be a great learning experience as you get accustomed to being authentic with other people. Be completely honest about your desires and needs, even when it might make you feel vulnerable. The only way you can get what you want is to let the chips fall where they may so that you'll learn from your mistakes and mistakes from others in return. It's important to take responsibility for what happens rather than blaming the person you love or the situation that's causing you stress or sadness in your life.
7. **Feel your emotions as they are:** Emotions aren't bad, and you don't have to deny them or keep them bottled up inside of you. Learn to understand the signs that your authentic self is trying to communicate to you through these emotions. As your awareness increases and the more in touch you are with the present moment and what's going on inside of yourself, you can be certain about what is real and what isn't. This will help you make better decisions as your authentic self takes over and guides the way

forward so that you're living a life that feels good, honest, authentic, and true.

Chapter 5: The Shadow and Relationships

The shadow can affect your relationships.
https://www.pexels.com/photo/photo-of-people-doing-fist-bump-3184430/

What are relationships? These are the connections that exist between two different people or parties. For the most part, when people talk about relationships, they're talking about romantic connections, but it's basically the way we relate with ourselves and those around us. So, technically, it's about romantic partnerships, family, friends, and coworkers. Relationships are about connection, usually rooted in emotion. You have a relationship with the world around you as long as you exist. Whether that relationship is warm or cold is a different matter entirely.

The impact of your shadow self can affect all areas of your life, including your relationships. How you relate with others and feel about yourself is in correlation with your shadow. It's not that other people are causing you to feel a certain way about yourself; you are unknowingly projecting negative characteristics onto people to protect yourself.

The Shadow in Marriage

A funny thing about marriage is that the things that draw a couple together in the first place are the same things that often turn out to be problematic later on. What was once attractive becomes rather repulsive. For instance, let's say a man was drawn to a woman's warmth and her ability to connect with people emotionally. Later on, he may think of her warmth and desire for connection as her being annoying and too much in his business. He may think of it as her being shallow and ingenuine in her affection.

When it comes to the woman, she may once have loved him because he was a dependable person whose reactions she could easily predict, who made her feel secure with him. Later on, she may come to look at those same qualities as him being quite the bore. She may consider his predictability as being set in his ways and stifling. So, it turns out that the things she once admired in him are the very things she loathes. The same qualities they both loved about each other are now relabeled and hated. What changed? Nothing - on the surface of things. However, both of them began to let their shadows take the reins and distort reality; this may be a cry for attention to the darkness that needs embracing in each person - and in the relationship itself.

How the Shadow Affects Your Relationships

If you're growing in love and intimacy with those who matter to you, it is important to get in touch with your shadow self. Shadow behavior causes you to relinquish responsibility for your part and blame other people for your situation and circumstances. When you're exhibiting shadow behavior, you're basically acting out based on the needs of your inner child, which were long ignored. It's what makes you want to isolate yourself and feel rage and depression. Often, those who haven't addressed their hidden anger and anxiety that bubbles beneath the surface will have to deal with their shadow self or face the consequences that do not positively affect the relationships in their lives.

Your shadow self can cause issues with your relationship by making you feel like you need to protect yourself from those you love whenever it's triggered. This is why you get into arguments that don't make sense or are difficult to resolve. Repression of your shadow's undesired aspects can lead you to act in ways that aren't true to who you really are. You've got a mask over your soul, which is not good for creating authentic relationships based on love and truth. When we're being inauthentic, the impulse is to run away from those who are healthy and have nothing but love for us because we think the worst parts of us are undeserving of their love.

For instance, if you're always hiding the bits of you that you're ashamed of, you'll find it impossible to relax. You'll always be on the lookout for something that might expose you and make you feel vulnerable; therefore, you avoid and run away before it gets close to you. When people want to get close, you prevent all forms of intimacy. You may not even know what blocks you have that make you continue acting the way you do. That's your shadow work. That's why you find it so hard to maintain relationships and why you keep running from others who want something deep with you, whether that's as friends, family, or romantic partners.

Locked within the shadow are the emotions of guilt and shame. You have to keep in mind that you are dealing with not one shadow *but two* when it comes to relationships. If both partners in a relationship, friendship, or family connection are unaware of the shadow self, it can be destructive and problematic. No matter the relationship in question, it is important for all parties to do the work of discovering their shadows and working with them. If you are single and are thinking about getting into a relationship, it would be best to sit down and work through your shadow issues before you connect with someone else. Otherwise, the chances that things will go from loving to toxic are quite high.

The Key to Healing Relationships

Choosing to understand your shadow is the first important step towards developing better relationships all around. What does it mean to know the traits you've hidden away from yourself? It's about observing your reactions and noticing when they come not from a place of love but from a darker place. It's also a good idea to notice when your partner acts out from their own shadow. When you become familiar with your shadow, you will notice that you no longer react without thinking, and your actions are rooted in compassion. You will notice that you and your partner are human beings deserving of respect and love and aren't simply meant to be used for each other's selfish ends.

To put this another way, getting friendly with your shadow will let you take part in your relationship in a healthy way. You simply must come to terms with the emotions, impulses, and needs that you've hidden. When you do, you'll be able to understand them with ease and notice when they arise. You'll also be able to communicate that to your partner, who, if they've got any understanding about shadow selves, will be able to help you. You'll realize that when it comes to dealing with shadows, it's a collaborative effort that requires being open and honest. There's no room for pointless ugly arguments.

Being in a relationship with someone can be a good thing because you can both act as a mirror for each other. The important thing is that you are both conscious of the importance of looking at your shadow aspects. You can use what you learn from your reflection as a tool to help you heal the parts that are still wounded.

Doing shadow work in your relationship is incredibly wholesome because it makes you compassionate towards each other. All that is required is for both partners to be willing and able to dig deep into their pasts and take a critical look at what they deeply fear. The more willing you are to face your shadows, the better your relationship will become because you can recognize other people's shadows and tolerate them far better than you used to. Don't waste another minute of your time blaming the other person for the fears you have not yet worked through and a past they can do nothing to change. Instead, bless them for the opportunity they have given you because they act as a mirror. This is how to develop healthy and long-lasting relationships.

A Guide to Working with the Shadow for Better Relationships

1. **Realize the difference between the shadow and the ego**: The shadow is what makes you who you are. It's also what makes you human as opposed to a robotic machine. The ego is all about being in your power and acting in a self-consistent, controlling, and self-serving manner. As long as the ego isn't falling apart on the inside, it can be controlled, repressed, or can be hidden away from

the world. But if your shadow begins to influence your behavior and decisions, it's time to take care of this part for yourself and others around you to begin to live an authentic life.

2. **Take care of yourself from the inside out:** As you begin to get in touch with the shadow side, you need to take care of yourself. This is about your emotional and spiritual health as much as anything else. You can't continue to just push things away or make excuses for what you, someone else, or a situation have done. Taking responsibility for everything, including your shadow side and your strengths and weaknesses, allows you to face what's going on inside of you and be honest about where you are today.

3. **Realize that no one is perfect:** The path of personal growth involves making mistakes and learning from them so that it's not a continual process. The shadow is the part of you that you aren't aware of when it comes to what you want and need or how you feel about others, situations, or even your behavior. Other people might also have a shadow, so they're not always as honest and open as you think they should be. This is why working with the shadow can benefit all of your relationships to some degree. Cut your partner some slack because they're not perfect either. Encourage them as they also work through their shadow issues.

4. **Accept the fact that life isn't fair:** The reality is that life isn't fair. People you have close relationships with will make mistakes, take advantage of others, and let their egos get in the way when convenient for them. To have a healthy relationship with others, you need to accept this reality. How they respond and act negatively is often more an indication of their issues than it is of you. So, when it comes to letting go of your expectations, don't blame them or feel victimized by them but begin to focus on yourself and what you can learn from them in the present moment.

5. **Let go of trying to control others:** You ultimately can't control the behavior of others. Therefore, it's best to focus on your behavior and how you can change it rather than trying to get others to change. The more you try to control someone else, the more they will act out, and the worse it will get between the two of you. It's better to let go of trying to control others and focus on changing yourself because this gives you something constructive to do

instead of blaming them for what they do or don't do.

6. **Get in touch with your anger:** Sometimes, when people have a shadow side, pent-up anger has built up inside them due to their circumstances growing up. This is even truer if they've been abused in some way. This can also happen if you've had your guilt and shame issues as a child. Getting in touch with your anger is about learning where this emotion stems from to embrace it, understand it, and use it to help you become more of who you are.

7. **Practice forgiveness:** When the anger builds up, try forgiving those who have hurt or betrayed your relationship. You might need to take this step before you forgive yourself and others for what happened because the process of forgiving someone else takes a great amount of work and is often uncomfortable times. Once you forgive, it'll give you a sense of freedom and will let you feel your authentic self more freely.

8. **Establish boundaries:** Setting boundaries is a way of maintaining and holding onto your integrity and being honest about what you need or don't need in your life. This also helps to let others know that this is part of who you are, so they understand you're not going to get manipulated or used. Suppose you don't establish boundaries early on with others. In that case, people will continue to take advantage of their power over you until it eventually becomes too much for either of you to handle.

9. **Accept that you're not perfect:** The biggest mistake that many people make when working on their personal growth is that they become too attached to perfection. If they don't achieve it or fall short of this, they feel like a failure, which is an unrealistic expectation to have. You need to be realistic about what you can and can't do and accept this as part of who you are so that you're not always trying to live up to an idealized version of yourself.

10. **Work towards becoming who you are:** When it comes to your shadow side, learn how to embrace it in a way that feels right for you. If you're more of a people-pleaser and find that your fears and anxieties are holding you back, you need to work on this part of yourself instead of just pushing it away. The more you work on your shadow side, the more honest and authentic you'll become. You will also feel less like a victim to your circumstances or other people's behaviors and actions in life.

11. **Learn from your mistakes:** You may have learned from your mistakes by accepting that you're not perfect and there's a reason for the things that have happened in your life. However, if you don't learn from them, the same mistakes will likely repeat themselves. This is why it's important to learn from each situation to take appropriate action and move forward with positivity.

Chapter 6: The Shadow and Society

Let's begin with talking about the meaning of society. According to the dictionary, society is defined as a group of people who live in a particular place and share certain beliefs or customs. Society is a collective way of living that has arisen from our need to cooperate and coexist with other people to survive. But what about the shadow self?

Research by psychologists and philosophers such as Sigmund Freud suggested that the human psyche can be divided into three parts: a person's ego (or conscious mind), an individual's darker self (often called their "shadow" or "id") where repressed emotions are kept, and desires take form, and finally, the person's superego (their moral guide). So how does society interact with these split personalities? Well, it does so through culture.

Culture refers to people's everyday beliefs and behaviors in a society that are passed down through generations. As you can imagine, culture also influences these three personalities as it sets guidelines for acceptable behaviors and thoughts.

So how does this play out in our day-to-day lives? Well, for example, let's imagine a situation where one person makes a mistake that puts the whole group in danger, so they are asked to apologize for their behavior. After doing so, the individual will begin to reflect on their actions and believe that they did something wrong for which they should be forgiven. Although the person may feel slightly guilty about having made a mistake, it is not a feeling that will prevent them from making similar mistakes in the future. So, what just happened to this person?

The answer is quite simple; they became integrated with society. As mentioned before, the culture encourages people to behave a certain way and have specific thoughts, which in this situation means that everyone expects an apology after someone makes a mistake. In this particular example, it could be a new person to the group, a member who is out of line, or their boss. Whatever the case may be, they will use society's "standards" to guide them along in their behavior.

You may have already seen this in action right outside your home where you live, because it is quite common for people to apologize for speeding when you are sitting on your front porch. However, this does not tell you how these words actually affect their thinking process. We do not realize that when we make an apology to our neighbors and family members, these words are working on our ego by seeding guilt into our psyche.

But why should we be responsible for our actions in this regard? Well, that is one of the themes often touched on with the shadow self. Society will tell you to make amends when you have done something wrong, but the shadow self will not believe this because these transgressions are its own fault – and not yours.

This is one of the main problems with the shadow because if you continue making mistakes, society will grow tired of them and eventually reinforce the shadow's belief that they are worthless. So, what happens if we try to move closer with society but still have our rejected parts hidden away? The answer lies within us and can be found in finding a balance between our ego, individual self, and superego.

How the Shadow Self Is Rooted in Childhood

One of the most interesting aspects of the shadow self is how it is made up of very un-conscious traits that are not even thought about until later in life when they begin to surface. In other words, our shadow selves result from what was learned and modeled by our parents, guardians, peers, and other members of society that we interacted with during childhood.

Every trait exists because it was learned during our formative years when we were too young to realize what was happening. If this is not enough to convince you, let's go over a few examples.

Many children believe that they are not important members of society, which manifests in them feeling like they have no friends or family to turn to in times of need. Children who have lived with a single parent or had an absent parent figure will often struggle with feeling like they are not getting enough attention or love. Some children grow up to believe that they are not important enough to have anything special because their parents did not give them any of the things they wanted or needed.

While it is easy to see how these examples could turn into destructive thinking, it is also possible for them to strengthen the ego. However, it is the combination of how successful we were growing up and what kind of person we grew into that determines which personality traits became part of our psyche. So, let's go back to our example from before, where one individual makes a mistake and must apologize for putting the group in danger.

If this person was successful growing up and made a name for themselves in their chosen field, they will accept the mistake, learn from it, and move on. However, if this person had a rough time growing up, their response would be quite different because they would feel like they didn't deserve to move up in society. This will prevent them from seeing the situation as one of learning but instead seeing it as a sign of something being wrong with them.

Although some people have what is called an "invisible" or "shadow" personality, it can easily be seen when a person cannot differentiate between right and wrong. This is because the ego will usually turn to the superego to determine what acceptable behavior is. If it cannot determine this on its own, it will become confused, which will result in the person feeling like they have no idea what they are doing.

This is why there is such a wide range of behaviors with these personalities because some will violate societal rules and be what others consider immoral while they feel that their actions are justified. Therefore, individuals with these personalities don't have a moral compass that can cause them to make choices based on their impulses. This makes them appear irrational and unpredictable, but appearances can be deceiving because, most of the time, these choices are being made out of fear.

There are different ways to interpret what the shadow self is, but there is one thing that cannot be denied, it exists within us. The only thing that it needs to be successful is time to grow into a personality. However, most of us will never get to see our shadow selves because they are hidden beneath layers of denial, sorrow, and anger.

We will never integrate with them and become whole because these traits will remain isolated and unacceptable in a world where your actions determine your worth. This is why many people live their lives without ever getting to know themselves, and it is also a big reason why some of us struggle with depressive disorders.

This does not mean you should become defensive when you find out about your shadow self because it will only worsen matters. Instead, you need to be objective and look at your behavior from an outside perspective to see if any traits could be labeled as unacceptable. Remember, this process should never be used as a means of self-flagellation; instead, it should be used to better understand who we are as human beings.

How to Reintegrate with the Shadow Self and Society

When it comes to self-reintegration, you will first need to take a fair look at yourself and make sure that you are not avoiding the problem. For this process to work, you'll need to help your shadow self understand you accept it as part of the whole. However, for this to be effective, there are a few things you need to know about your shadow self.

The first thing is that it has a mind of its own and will act independently regardless of what we want or say. The second thing is that you'll only become complete when you accept all parts of yourself, including those you hate. Those who hate themselves will avoid anything that makes them feel negative, so they often carry on in life without knowing their true thoughts and feelings.

Therefore, they can't know what it means to be complete with every part of themselves because they have abandoned their shadow selves to shield themselves from experiencing pain. Now let's discuss a few ways you can help your shadow self become a part of your personal identity so you can find your place in society in healthier ways.

Recognize your hidden traits. Others hold the clues you seek: Most individuals with a shadow self do not know how many traits they have until the right situation arises. Therefore, when you recognize your hidden traits, it will be an enlightening experience for you. The next time you meet someone and have the rare chance to know more about them, pay attention to what they say about themselves and their thoughts. If you hear something that does not seem like it would fit with who you think they are, then there is a good chance that part of your shadow self is talking through them. Therefore, take the time to listen to what they say because it could be a clue as to what traits make up *your* shadow side.

Change your beliefs: If you want to discover more about yourself, a few things must occur before this. For starters, you will need to develop a clean slate mentality and start taking a hard look at your beliefs. In addition, you'll need to let go of any judgmental behaviors to become open to the things happening around you. When you do this, the next time society judges you for something and causes your shadow self to feel negative emotions; it will find an outlet for those emotions. Finally, when you learn how to accept and change your beliefs to match who you are as a person, there is no telling what kind of life we could lead.

Step into the person you want to be: While your shadow self will not really have a choice about accepting you, it is possible that you may need to prove yourself willing to accept it before it will hear you out and stop sabotaging you. Therefore, there are certain things that you can do to make sure that your shadow self knows that you are serious about becoming a part of yourself. For starters, you'll need to eliminate any fears and make sure that you have no reservations about going after what it wants for you. To do this, start working towards becoming who you want to be and stop thinking so much about how others might judge your actions.

No personality cannot be broken down into the three categories we have discussed above. When it comes to revealing our shadow selves, it is usually not a pleasant experience because most of us do not want to face the things which make us feel like we are "less than." However, when you learn how to look at yourself objectively, you'll find that you don't have to hide from yourself anymore to become whole again.

The Shadow and Self Sabotage

The shadow self should not be feared because it is a part of us that we all possess. The only thing we need to fear is the self-sabotage that happens when we neglect our shadow selves and refuse to acknowledge their existence. When this happens, the negative traits of our shadow selves will be isolated and eventually forgotten for good. This means that those who let the negative aspects of their personalities run amok will suffer from depression, anxiety, self-harm, and feelings of hopelessness, just to name a few. Though it might be difficult to face who we really are, it is far more painful to live a life where negative traits run wild.

Everyone will eventually come in contact with their shadow self, and the only way they will be able to know how to react to that contact is by knowing what makes up the shadow self. How does the shadow self sabotage you?

It will make you feel unworthy of what you want in life: This can lead to depression and, if left unchecked, will eventually lead to self-destructive behaviors. It causes you to have a low opinion of yourself, making you feel like nothing is ever good enough. The shadow self makes us believe that we are incapable of achieving what we desire out of life, which allows our negative traits to run wild without the proper guidance necessary to control them.

It will involve you in unhealthy relationships: When you are unaware of the negative traits which comprise your shadow self, you'll often find yourself in relationships with people who make you feel bad about yourself. When this occurs, the only place these negative feelings will go is into your shadow self, creating a vicious cycle of strengthening your shadow's stranglehold on your life.

It will make you sabotage your happiness: Sometimes, when we are unhappy with parts of ourselves, the shadow may decide that the only way to make ourselves feel better is by making others around us feel bad about themselves or by doing something to harm them. This can often be done by acting mean to the people we love and belittling them so that we can feel better about ourselves. This is a terrible way for the shadow to react because it does not create the best conditions for you to reach your full potential.

It will sabotage your relationship with others: Our shadow can lead us to become resentful towards others and make us feel angry at them. When you get angry, you often take actions that make the other person feel worse about themselves and make them question their worth. Sometimes, the wrongs your shadow perceives aren't even actual wrongs, and these innocent people may be completely unaware of having slighted you!

It can sabotage your finances: When you struggle to balance out your finances and try hard to secure your future, it is often because the shadow is trying to sabotage your life. This happens because when we are constantly reminded of our shortcomings, we often think out of fear that nobody would want us, and our talents and skills will be wasted or are not as great as we'd like to think. We feel hopeless about our employment prospects or spend money on unnecessary purchases, which only compounds our money problems.

The shadow self can also cause health problems: Ignoring your shadow can wreak havoc on your physical, mental, and spiritual health. It can manifest as a chronic health issue and can compound the matter by leading you to make decisions that only serve to exacerbate your health problems.

You could even assume you're doing the right things for your condition but not realize you're being lied to the precise choices that will keep the problem around for a long time.

It will cause you to believe that you don't deserve the things you have: When things are going well, your shadow self will find ways to convince you that you do not deserve the good things you're experiencing. It could turn out disastrous for you if you eventually listen to that voice. You may find yourself rejecting offers that would actually be good for you, for the most logical sounding reasons that beneath the surface are actually your shadow self grasping at any excuse to keep you from what you want.

For instance, you could have a life-changing meeting tomorrow and be all excited about it, but for some reason, you decide to have a tub of ice cream the night before, knowing fully well that you are lactose intolerant. But you think to yourself, "Oh, it's just this one time, and I'm celebrating! I deserve this!" Next thing you know, tomorrow rolls around, and your stomach is so messed up you can't even get out of bed. This is just one of the ways the shadow can sabotage you.

Shadow Work, Sabotage, and Society

From the previous section, you can see how with an unintegrated shadow, it can be hard to find your place in society when the shadow continues to thwart your best efforts at every turn. Whether you're about to cement your place in the world with a new job, a new project, or a new set of relationships that would be amazing for you, you might find it really challenging to do any of these things successfully if you haven't called your shadow by its name and chosen to address it.

It's possible to even seem "well-integrated" into society on the surface and still struggle with feelings of lack of self-worth. You could "belong" and yet feel like you don't really belong. There's nothing weird about that. It's your shadow convincing you of your lack of worth. So if you think you don't need to do shadow work because society accepts you, you'd be very wrong. The fact that society accepts you means that you've fitted yourself into its standards and buried certain aspects of yourself that society isn't okay with. However, you can't bury those parts of yourself, no matter how much you try. They will be still there, in the shadow.

Doing shadow work will help you find your place in society without feeling sell-out because you'll be able to have better boundaries around where you begin and end. As important as it is to be a part of it, you don't want to lose yourself in the process because if you do, rest assured your shadow will have lots to say about that, and you're not going to like it. Shadow work is vital so you can feel like you're an authentic person, true to the values you hold dear as an individual – while understanding your worth to society.

A Guide to Bringing Your Shadow to the Surface

Know that the shadow is always with you: Whether you're aware of it or not, your shadow is always with you and constantly has your back. You don't feel as though it's a part of you because the light is so intense that it blinds the shadow into hiding itself. It may seem like the light and dark are in complete opposition to each other, but they're not. They exist side by side in perfect harmony and balance. Remind yourself of this fact, and it will be more than enough to help you bring it to the forefront of your consciousness.

Keep a detailed journal, and reflect on your feelings at every day's end: The more you reflect on what you feel in the light when you wake up in the morning and how those feelings change throughout the day, the more you'll begin to understand where the shadow vibration comes from. When you know that your shadow is always there with you, making decisions for you in the background, regardless of whether it is feeding into what is happening or not, it will be easier to know it's time to bring it out into the light. It's not going to come out on its own.

Listen to the voice and embrace its purpose: The important thing when dealing with a negative self-image or feeling unworthy is not to reject the shadow's voice but instead listen to its intent and receive it emotionally. You can do this by asking it to show you things you are worthy of. You'll be surprised at the things that come up when you ask.

Ask for your light to surround and heal the shadow: As you learn how to work with your shadow and bring it into the light, you must call on your higher self and other spiritual teachers to help heal it back into full alignment with you. If you don't believe in anything, you could meditate. Your shadow will need love and compassion, which is what your light vibration brings. All shadows are worthy of healing, just as all emotions are worthy of love and compassion. Let this be a reminder that no matter what your shadow does or says, apply love to raise its vibration in alignment with yours.

Chapter 7: Shadow Work Exercises

Shadow work is the exploration of your dark side, which isn't easy to spot. You can do shadow work on your own or with a therapist. Some people take the help of psychedelics as well, but that is beyond the scope of this book. Considering all you now know about the shadow, I bet you're more than glad to know that there's something you can do to become more aware of it, grow enough to stop letting it sabotage you, and also help you dig into the good that hides within it, like talents you may not be aware of.

Shadow work is a concept of having different aspects of ourselves and the banished parts with which we're trying to reconcile. When you choose to explore your shadow, you'll find many answers to questions that have plagued you for years about why you act the way you do and why, despite your best efforts, you've been unable to change or maintain change for long. As you do shadow work, you'll develop a stronger and deeper relationship with your authentic self and your soul, which means you'll become a fuller, grander, more ideal version of yourself.

What You Should Know About Shadow Work

You need to know that shadow work isn't something you jump right into and call it done within minutes. You're going to need to put in some time and effort, learning how to notice your emotions because you may have a habit of shrugging them off, which doesn't bode well for shadow work. You must pay attention to the way you react to things, and you've got to be intentional, which can take time. So, the more you do the work, the better you get at doing this.

If you're new to shadow work, it's a good idea to have a journal or a logbook to note the times and situations when you have intense reactions and emotions and write down the triggers for you. Can you think of times when your breathing got shallow, your head felt hot and heavy, or you felt like you just got sucker-punched in the gut? Those are the reactions you should start noticing. Maybe you also tend to get itchy and sweaty in certain situations. Note it all down, along with what's going on with you at the moment. You need to pay attention to these strong emotions because they're basically your shadow revealing itself. When you can note the emotions, you'll start to notice the patterns around them.

By doing Shadow work, you'll notice many layers within you. Pause for a moment and consider the times when you felt an emotion welling up in you to a point where you almost succumbed to it – and you tried so hard to figure out why you were reacting so strongly. You feel the way you do because an aspect of you has been dying to come out for a while, and it's no longer willing to be silenced. So, rather than shoving them back down, it's best to take a moment and think about what they could mean. Face your demons.

Notice that when we come across something, we have a tendency to make snap judgments and shut it all down. However, the more you judge yourself, the larger your shadow looms, and the more you rip yourself apart. Sit with your emotions instead. Before you get into shadow work, ask yourself:

1. Who are you?
2. What do you want?
3. What do you need to release to make your dreams real?
4. Who's the person you need to grow into to be worthy of those things?
5. How would you like to present yourself to the world?

We're about to get into the various shadow work exercises. Note that you can do them first thing in the morning or at night before sleeping. If you can't show up at these times, it's okay to do them whenever you have the time, but the important thing is to do them every day. You will need about fifteen minutes for each exercise.

Voice Dialogue

You may need: a journal and a sound recorder.

A journal will help you with the voice dialogue method.

https://www.pexels.com/photo/ball-point-pen-on-opened-notebook-606541/

With this exercise, you're acknowledging that your psyche is split into two basic aspects: the primary selves, and the rejected selves, the latter being the shadow and all things you've continued to treat as repulsive and undesirable. The primary aspects are the parts of you that you've developed to keep you safe in how you present yourself to others, which means that the creation and amplification of this aspect will lead to your unwanted parts.

Let's assume your primary self is someone who doesn't brag. That means your rejected self knows how to brag and enjoys it. So, here's how the voice dialogue exercise would work.

1. You're going to conduct interviews, asking questions of your primary self, the part of you that won't brag. To do this, you have to completely embody the person who never brags and describe how you see bragging. Ask questions like, what's it like to brag? What do you think of people you see bragging? Don't hold back in your answers. How long have you always considered bragging being undesirable? What's the earliest you recall thinking of braggarts this way? What do you think the consequences of

bragging are? You can ask these and any other questions that come to mind.

2. As you ask these questions, please make sure you're validating this primary self. You want it to feel like you understand it and support it because it's a valid part of you that you created due to people not approving of you talking about your accomplishments. You could allocate anywhere from ten to thirty minutes for this part. Following these questions, the part you've suppressed will find it easier to come out and play. Then you'll be able to experience yourself as a braggart, and that will bring you to the conclusion that while you may have suppressed that part of you, it is still alive and well.

3. Interview this repressed self in the same way that you interviewed the primary self. Make sure to validate this aspect of yourself and allow it to brag. Acknowledge that it's part of you, and it's going to be much easier to be at peace with the act of bragging no matter where you encounter it. You can note down your answers in a journal or simply record them on your phone to review later if you wish.

Standing Up to Your "Good" Self

You will need: a journal to note your observations

If you're like most people, you probably think of yourself as a good person. Most of us do. The thing about shadow work is that for all the deliberate goodness we demonstrate, there's an opposite "badness" within us that balances it out, even though we've learned to repress it.

For instance, a person may consider themselves to be very meticulous and organized. It is a good thing and nothing to be ashamed of, but there's nothing wrong with not being put together either.

1. If you truly think of yourself as being organized, pause and ask yourself if you really are that way all the time.

2. Acknowledge that there are times when you're not as great at being organized, and you'll be able to make peace with it. The more you adamantly insist that you're organized and efficient, the more you repress and reject the part of you that isn't. That just feeds your shadow, giving it more power to come up and challenge you in the most unexpected and inconvenient ways possible. You have to be willing to embrace this part of yourself.

3. Make a list of all the things about yourself you consider to be true, and go through that list to acknowledge that there is a counterparty that exists to match everything you think of as who you really are.
4. Be at peace with the other aspects, and accept them without judgment.

Shadow Work Meditation

Meditation is a great way to learn about your emotions and their root causes. It can also help you learn to accept yourself more than you ever could without it. With meditation, all you need is yourself and a quiet place where you won't be bothered for ten to fifteen minutes.

1. Sit in a comfortable position you can maintain for the duration, and just pay attention to your breath.
2. If you notice that your attention has wandered away, you can simply come back to your breath without beating yourself up.
3. For each time you get distracted, accept that and bring your attention back to your breath.

Getting distracted multiple times in a session happens even to the best of meditators, so don't be mad at yourself for experiencing that. In fact, you should be thankful because the more you notice you're distracted, the better this practice will be for you because you're building awareness. This awareness will translate to noticing when your shadow rears its head and is about to sabotage you.

You'll create mental space between your words and actions and the impulses that cause them so that you can evaluate your choices before making them. Also, learning to do nothing but be in the here and now will teach you how to integrate the aspects of you that you don't accept right now.

You'll learn non-judgment and acceptance because you'll have thoughts flowing into your mind as you meditate. You just have to notice the thoughts but return to the breath. Don't judge the thoughts, don't criticize, or analyze them. Simply let them flow out the way they came in. You'll be able to notice your shadow self and, for once, try to accept it as it is, without judging. When you accept the shadow, it will no longer compulsively place roadblocks on the path to your success.

3-2-1

You may need: A journal and/or a sound recorder.

This is a method crafted by Ken Wilber, and you can either work with it as a meditation or use it in a journal. It is called the 3-2-1 method because there are three steps to do.

1. Face the issue.
2. Speak to the issue.
3. Embody it.

How does this work? You're going to take a look at something that isn't going well in your life, such as a problematic relationship with someone, and use that to gain some much-needed insight that will help you be more rational in your thoughts rather than overwhelmed by your emotional reactions.

1. **Face the issue:** Step one is to figure out who or what it is you're going to focus on in this exercise. It's usually better to do this with someone you're struggling to maintain a healthy connection with, but this doesn't always have to be the case. It's not an easy thing to be in the same space as someone you might not be able to stand, whether out of anger, spite, or lust. Or a feeling of being inferior. However, that will make this exercise worthwhile, so pick someone you react to strongly regarding emotions.

    Imagine the situation or a person in your mind's eye. Do your best to recreate what they look like. If it's a situation, do your best to replay it in your mind. When you accurately represent the person or situation, you should home in on the emotions they bring within you. You can either use your journal for this or speak your words aloud. Address them in the third person and talk about the things about them that you love or hate or are most drawn to or repulsed by. It's important that you don't think too much about what you want to say or journal. Just feel the way you feel and immediately put that feeling to words. You shouldn't censor yourself. Let it all out as it is; there's no one to judge you. Use third-person pronouns when you do this part of the exercise.

2. **Speak to the issue:** Now it's time to address the situation or person as if they're happening or standing right in front of you. Make use of the pronoun "you." You can journal or speak. For this portion

of the exercise, you can ask the following questions, among anything else you want:

- Do you know that this is the way you make me feel?
- Why do you treat me this way?
- What is it that you want the most from me?
- What is the lesson that you want me to finally learn?

With each question, pause, and listen. You're going to get an answer. You can say the answer aloud if you want or simply note them down in your little journal. If you're inspired to ask more questions, go ahead. Also, notice if the projection you've created has more to say other than the answers they've given you.

3. **Embody it:** Now, this isn't necessarily a comfortable thing to do, but it is an essential step. The traits and issues you've been avoiding are who you are, and it's time to fill those shoes. You need to become who you've been facing and speaking to. You're going to revisit the sentences you made in the first step to describe the problematic person or situation that your shadow has projected onto. This time, you're going to replace the third person pronouns with the pronouns "I" and "me." So, you might find yourself saying things like "I am annoying," "I am proud," or "I am scared." It isn't comfortable, again, but this is how you connect your conscious and unconscious aspects to finally feel balance and peace within you. You have to acknowledge that all of this is within you.

Now, to be clear, this is not meant to make you feel ashamed of yourself. You can accept that you're annoying or angry without feeling guilty about it or feeling like you have to hide your head. It's about accepting those truths about you while being compassionate. You should also extend the same feeling of compassion to the situation or person you addressed during the exercise.

Shadow Mirror Work Affirmations

You will need: a journal and a mirror.

You can also work with shadow work affirmations using a mirror. Unlike regular affirmations, shadow work affirmations won't always be happy and full of sunshine and rainbows. Some of them are meant to keep you grounded. The following are some of the affirmations you can use to help you deal with your shadow healthily. Make sure you're looking into your eyes with love and compassion using a mirror, and feel every word and what it means to you. Please note that you may fight them the first time you run through these. That's okay, but the statement's truth will hit you with time, and you'll be wiser for it. Here are the affirmations:

1. I will never get the parenting I'd have liked as a kid, and I'm at peace with that.
2. I can accept that while I'm special, I'm no more special than others.
3. I cannot claim responsibility for what happened in my childhood, but I'm grown up now and in charge of how I handle it now.
4. What they did to me caused me pain, but they did the best they knew to do at the time.
5. I have decided to always forgive because I have realized that's the path to peace.
6. I now accept that we're all able to build and destroy, love, and hate. And that's why we all deserve to be forgiven and shown mercy.
7. I can understand being bitter, but I now accept that it's not worth it and doesn't serve me.
8. I've made mistakes, but I'm not made of just mistakes. What matters is how I choose to make things right.
9. I'm at peace with the fact that I have made and will make mistakes. I also accept that I can always do better.
10. There are those who seek love through selfish and hurtful ways, and they need love the most.
11. I only need to be approved of and respected by one person, and that's me.
12. If I'm in a toxic situation or relationship, that's my choice. I'm free to walk away from it when I can find it in me to do so.
13. Any relationship or situation that makes me feel drained isn't worth my energy and time.
14. Other people's opinions of me aren't my concern.
15. While it feels good to have other people's approval, their approval means nothing in the end.
16. I am at home with all my imperfections

17. Having a terrible background doesn't excuse my terrible attitude. It drives me to be better.
18. I always see ways to improve, and I'm happy to learn every day.
19. I won't seek validation under the guise of looking for "feedback" or other input.
20. I alone am responsible for my happiness.

You can choose one affirmation to work with each day for fifteen minutes at a time, or you can work through all of these affirmations per session. It's your call.

Chapter 8: The Ups and Downs of Shadow Work

You might be completely aware that you have things to work on but feel totally overwhelmed by the prospect of doing so. It's much easier to ignore it in the hopes that it goes away, but sometimes there will be a price to pay for not dealing with shadows in your life.

You might have noticed that when you take something away, something else gets added into the mix. When you learn to be more open and honest about your weaknesses, you'll get many opportunities to love and accept yourself as an imperfect human being. You'll learn how valuable you are as a person. There will be many ups and downs as you do shadow work, but it will be worth it.

Benefits of Shadow Work

You'll be forced to deal with the issue of your shadow self: As long as you're unwilling to learn about your shadows, you'll continue to have them. That makes you a victim of circumstance, and it doesn't mean that you have lost control as long as you know what is going on. Learning about your shadows will help free up some space in your mind where something new can become a glue that holds it all together. You go from being a victim of circumstances to an active participant in making things happen the way they should.

You're no longer living in the dark: You'll have clarity on where you stand concerning your life. You'll be able to discern your values and know what is important to you without being confused by your dark side. This will help you make better decisions about how you want to show up in life from now on, but you must open up and become vulnerable to what comes. The process of bringing your shadow into the light is not easy or always pleasant, but if you value your mental health, spiritual growth, and emotional well-being, then working with it will give you those things.

You will learn how to bring love and compassion into your life: If you've been beating yourself up for far too long, shadow work will help you learn to love yourself better. You'll stop being hard on yourself and begin to understand that what you thought was so wrong with you is actually not as bad as it seems. Choosing to do the work means you're going to realize you have no choice but to see your shadow side as worthy of love and acceptance, and this is a good thing for you because you'll also attract love from all around you.

You will have a better relationship with yourself: When you learn everything about yourself that makes you feel unworthy or unlovable, you'll develop the ability to embrace this new information and use it to improve yourself. As you begin to see your shadow as a good thing, it will begin to change in ways you never imagined. That's when you'll learn how to love yourself and the world around you.

You will be able to resolve feelings of anger and hostility: As you find out why you have so much anger in your life, it will help heal the source by providing a way for forgiveness and making amends for the wrongs that happened in the past. It doesn't mean that it will be easy, but it does mean that if you work through the process with an open mind, there will be healing along the way as things fall into place just as they should be.

You'll have an easier time making decisions: As you learn to see a larger picture of your life, you'll be able to make better decisions. You won't be running on blind faith because you'll have a far better idea of what is best for you and your life. It will become easier for you to trust yourself and follow through with your direction in life.

You'll manage to stay out of trouble: When you learn how to work with your shadow and start becoming a more spiritual person, you'll find yourself surrounded by people who are moving in the same direction as you. As you learn to love yourself after all these years of self-abuse, others will recognize that and become curious about what makes you different from them, but more than that, you will no longer be a magnet for trouble and drama.

Challenges of Doing Shadow Work

You must be willing to confront your inner darkness and bring it into the light: This is not going to be easy, and it may not be pleasant, but if you strongly believe in something greater than yourself and a willingness to explore your true potential, you'll eventually get what you need out of this process. Your faith in yourself will have to be strong enough for you to come out on top with less pain than you might experience otherwise.

Tip: Open up and let yourself be vulnerable with whatever comes. It does not mean you'll have to share what you know about yourself with everyone, but you might need someone who can provide a safe place for reflective self-examination. If you don't have a counselor or other professional that supports your needs, find someone who can give you the kind of support you need to get through this challenging process.

You will have to be willing to change your ways: Having healthy boundaries will help you in this regard. If you're willing to let go of negative patterns that have been haunting you for years, it will become easier to conquer them. You must be willing to grow beyond your comfort zone. It's easy to stay within your little world of self-controlling and self-pity, but once you get beyond that and allow yourself to embrace life with all its ups and downs, the process of embracing your shadow will become a lot easier on you. You'll have areas of comfort where the outside world has no place because that's how it should be if you want to be happy. Many people struggle to change the way they've always behaved and the habits that have become ingrained in their way of being.

Tip: Keep in mind that this is the hardest part of a new life and accept it. Be willing to do some soul searching as you go along and embrace new ideas, perspectives, or ways of living.

You will need to look within yourself: The only way to see everything that is going on with your shadow is from within yourself. When you notice yourself acting a certain way or doing things out of character, it usually means there is something for you to learn about yourself. It could be a behavior you want to change or a way of thinking that you want to understand better. We all have a dark side, and depending on how we feel about ourselves, it can take us in different directions. It's okay to be afraid and get help if you need it. You don't have to do this alone.

Tip: If things about yourself are difficult to accept, it's time to face them head-on and deal with them somehow. There's no way out but through.

You must be willing to face the truth about yourself: People tend to run from the truth because they are uncomfortable with it. If you're willing to look at yourself through your eyes and learn as much as you can from the situation, you'll find things will become clearer and easier to handle. For this process to work, you must be willing to do what is necessary for yourself. If what is needed here is the truth about yourself, nobody else can make that happen except for you. You must be willing to confront your feelings without being too hard on yourself, and that may take a little time and patience. Some things can't be hidden from yourself any longer, and once they're out in the open, it becomes all too apparent what you need to do about them.

Tip: You don't have to love this part of yourself, but you do have to accept it for what it is and work with it somehow as you move forward with your life.

You need to be patient with yourself: In the beginning, you'll feel like this is the hardest thing to do, and you'll wonder why you took it on in the first place. However, as time goes on and you face one challenge after another, things will become easier for you. You're going to take one step at a time as you walk through this process, and if it's not entirely clear how it will unfold for you in the end, just keep putting one foot in front of the other until something happens that brings further clarity into your life.

Tip: Keep moving forward slowly but surely and do what feels right for yourself. With any new habit or way of life, it takes time for the past patterns to fall away, and in their place come new opportunities for growth and change. This is a long-term process, so give yourself time to evolve, grow, and become someone you want to be.

You will, at some point, have to forgive yourself: As it turns out, this is something many people struggle with as they try to change their lives because they're so hard on themselves and don't realize that forgiveness is what allows them to move forward and become new. When you forgive yourself, other things start to fall away as well. You have to be willing to let go of self-loathing and see yourself from a new perspective. As hard as it might be for you, let go of what has hurt you in the past to come out on the other side happy and unencumbered by your past mistakes.

Tip: Forgiveness is not always easy, but when it comes from within, a deep sense of peace settles over you. It's important for your good to learn to forgive yourself for any mistakes that have held you back in the past.

You must trust the process: Whatever process you're going through and however long it takes to get to where you want to be, it's important to trust it. It means having utmost belief and faith that whatever is going on with you will work itself out. It might not be entirely clear at first how any of this happened or what role certain people played in your life, but over time things will become clearer, and the changes will take place. It is not an easy task, and most people don't have the patience for it, so they give up when things don't happen fast enough. Take your time with this, and trust that life will bring into play what's right for you when the time is right.

Tip: If you don't trust yourself, it will be hard to take the journey toward your dark side. You have to trust yourself and your instincts enough to go with the flow as you try to make changes in your life. If you listen to others who try to stop you, you'll only delay progress since they won't know what is right for you any more than you do. Your higher self knows what is best for you, so let that part of yourself direct your journey into the unknown. Let go of fear and embrace what life brings with open arms and a willingness to learn from it no matter how painful or frightening it might be.

As David Schoen puts it in War of the Gods in Addiction, "The more cut off and unconscious we are of our personal shadows, the more vulnerable we are to having those shadows break out and be set free for a time by addictive behaviors." So regardless of your challenges, always remember that it's worth it in the end.

How to Navigate the Ups and Downs of Shadow Work

1. **Face your fears:** The biggest obstacle we all face as we try to navigate our shadow is the fear of what might happen if we allow ourselves to see where it really lives. We stand in denial and pretend there isn't any reason to be afraid because everything that has happened to us in the past is "just terrible." The reality is that the bulk of who we are has been formed from our experiences, and it's not going anywhere any time soon.

2. **Trust your instincts:** One thing that's not easy to do when you're trying to move into the shadow is to trust your instincts and forget everything you've been taught about being a good person. Actually, it's even harder than that because we have been told by our parents and society in general that there are certain things we can't do and may very well end up harming others if we don't follow the rules. We're taught to keep one foot in front of the other as we walk through life because all too often, life doesn't fall into place for us or meet all our expectations because of our "weaknesses." So, while we ignore our doubts, we deny the value of what is inside of us. We have no idea how important it is to explore who we are and accept the gifts that come with it, even though we might not understand what they are or why they're revealed at this time.

3. **Stop trying at all costs:** If you want to move into your shadow and follow the path of change and growth, you must stop trying to be someone else and just be yourself. Once you accept that person is who you really are deep inside, it won't be long before you begin to see the world differently. You can't control what will happen because many things in life aren't meant to happen the way the plan is laid out. When you stop trying and just let things happen, new doors open up for you that have been closed for years.

Chapter 9: Bringing the Shadow into the Light

Bringing the shadow into light.
Wittylama, CC BY-SA 4.0 <https://creativecommons.org/licenses/by-sa/4.0>, via Wikimedia Commons: https://commons.wikimedia.org/wiki/File:Shadows_on.jpg

If the shadow is everything that we've repressed, then it stands to reason that the light is the part of us we've accepted. If the shadow sabotages us, then the light is our strength. If the shadow has taken over our lives, the light shines through to set us free. When we start the process of accepting our shadow, the next step is to bring it into the light where we can begin to live life on a new level. If you're willing to do this, you can get your life back and experience all that's possible for you in this lifetime.

Make no mistake as you see your shadow emerging in every aspect of your life. You'll be horrified by what is happening but, at the same time, thrilled to be alive. You'll realize that while you may not have all the answers, there is a power within you that has never been tapped before.

As this force emerges and changes your life in ways you could never dream were possible, you'll feel as if a part of you has been awakened from a long, deep sleep. You'll begin to see yourself in ways that go far beyond anything you've experienced before, as if there's so much more for you to learn about being happy and living life full-out. If this is the path for you, take your time and do things right, or it won't last. You have to be patient but also determined enough to see it through when times get tough because they will.

Draining vs. Energizing

This is a short and sweet exercise where you can figure out what your daily experiences are doing to your psyche. Here's what you need to do:

1. Get a pen and a piece of paper.
2. Create two columns.
3. Name column a "Draining" and column b "Energizing."
4. Consider the interactions that you go through daily.
5. Any interactions that drain you go to column a.
6. Put the stuff that energizes you in column b.
7. Figure out how you can begin to cut down on the stuff in the column.
8. You can do this for situations as well. It doesn't just have to be interactions.

Speak Aloud

Another way to bring your shadow to the light is to discuss it with someone you can trust and who has your best interests. They should be able to help you so you don't feel ashamed of yourself and do much better at accepting yourself as you are.

1. With what you've learned so far from this book, identify the shadow aspects you have.
2. Speak about these aspects with a trusted friend or a licensed therapist.
3. Talk about these aspects. For instance, you could find that you want to feel capable but were taught to only rely on others, even for the smallest things.
4. Go deep into the impact this belief has had on your life.
5. Talk about the different ways you could work with and integrate those aspects of your life.

Rainbow Bright Healing Tube

This is a powerful technique to show your dark side in your dreams. Everything you've ever suppressed will likely show up, so be sure you're ready for what's to come. When you have those dreams, pause to think that whatever you're afraid of isn't that bad. Here's what you need to do:

1. Sit in a comfy chair or lie on a mat or on your bed.
2. Close your eyes and breathe deliberately, allowing each inhale to flow into each exhale.
3. In your mind's eye, picture a rainbow. Make it the brightest one you've ever seen.
4. Visualize that rainbow encompassing your body like a tube. Notice how the colors glow even brighter than they were at the start.
5. Feel the colors of the rainbow go through you. Play with them like a kid.
6. Remain in this tube for five to ten minutes, or as long as possible, then go to bed or end the session.

Write a Letter

Every emotion is energy, whether you term it good or bad. No one on Earth is above getting carried away by the so-called *bad emotions* like worry, frustration, rage, anxiety, fear, etc. The trouble is, when most people experience these emotions, they would rather shove them down than go through them. Because we have been taught ever since we were little that certain emotions are simply not okay to demonstrate, even if justified. By now, you were well aware of the fact that that energy does not disappear; *it goes straight to the shadow.* The exercise of writing a love letter to your shadow is an excellent way to get in touch with it and bring some light and healing to it. Here's what you need to do.

1. **Pick a shadow aspect to deal with:** You have to decide which aspect you want to bring light to. Could it be your fear of being seen by others or your fear of scarcity? Perhaps you'd like to address the self-doubt that cripples you. Or you'd like to address the self-sabotage that has hindered you from attaining the heights you should. Whatever you like to address, make sure that you are specific. For instance, you can't just address the emotion of fear. Narrow it down. Fear of what, exactly.

2. **Get your paper:** At the very top, just as you'd start off an informal letter, say, "Dear [Name of Shadow Aspect]. Make sure to feel the emotion behind the word "dear" because you're trying to pull it close to you and shine love and light on it. So, beware of the temptation to be snarky in intent as you write that.

3. **Thank the Shadow Aspect:** The next line should begin with, "Thank you." Go ahead and thank this shadow aspect for everything that you understand. It's been created to keep you safe from or lead you towards. For instance, if you are dealing with the fear of death, you can thank this fear for keeping you protected from all sorts of harm and making sure that you stay alive. There is nothing to be afraid of when it comes to fear. It can be quite a positive emotion, but the trouble is most people don't think of it that way. When it comes to working with your shadow, keep in mind that no energy or emotion is totally bad or good. The trouble with fear is not fear itself but the fact that we continue to ignore and suppress it and act like it is a shameful thing to feel it. If you pause to give this thought, you will find that fear has benefited you.

4. **Note down the ways this shadow aspect has been beneficial to you:** Now that you realize nothing is entirely good or evil, you can think of the different ways your shadow aspect has helped you and write them down. Make sure to come up with at least two different benefits it has offered you.

5. **Pay attention to the shifts within you as you write:** You may sense a shift in your thought process, energy levels, or emotions. Pay attention to your chest area and shoulders in particular. You may notice a reduction of tension and easier breathing, or it could be a

warm sensation flooding your body. Note all the sensations you feel at the end of the letter, or if you prefer, on a different page. As you do this, it is important to recall that the letter is one of love because your shadow is not your enemy; it is simply an underappreciated friend that you're only beginning to realize has been of great service to you in the best ways it knew.

Challenges of Bringing Your Shadow into the Light

Consistency is not the easiest thing, but you must stick with the process: Just as the shadow emerges in stages, so will your experience of the light work. Whatever you may have experienced in the past, it's unlikely that you'll experience it again. At first, this feels like a letdown, but we have to maintain a certain level of commitment and trust that everything will unfold on its schedule. Remember, this process isn't an overnight thing. The one thing that helps me with this is recalling just how fortunate I am to know what I know about myself now compared to when I was younger. How have I made this much progress with my shadow? By staying consistent with the work.

Tip: Do not think of this as a one-time thing, but as a lifestyle of getting to know yourself. Consider yourself a lifelong explorer of your consciousness, and it won't feel so overwhelming.

You will be in pain: Learn to embrace the pain from the process. It's not a choice to be made lightly, though it is *precisely* why you need to take this journey. If you want to bring your shadow into the light, you'll have to give up many familiar things. You must stop looking outside yourself for answers to see who is inside. Your fears and doubts can seem overwhelming at first, but they will turn out to be beautiful gifts if we allow them to be part of our lives. You can't experience significant change without some pain, and bringing your shadow into the light is no different.

Tip: While you may want to run away from the pain and confusion, the fact remains that you'll be much better for having gone through all those emotions. Do not tempt yourself to remain where you are unless you're willing to continue to live a limited life. When it gets tough, remember that as you continue to bravely plant one foot in front of the other, it will be worth it.

You will feel vulnerable: Everyone experiences vulnerability as they begin to surrender to the process of self-acceptance. You can't keep your walls up and down at the same time. You'll have to let a few of them down even if they're hard to let go of. The more walls you're willing to take down, the easier it will be for you to bring your shadow into the light.

Tip: Remember just how vulnerable we all are as human beings, and that vulnerability makes us beautiful and brings us closer to others. We are entitled to those feelings because we all feel them at some point. Allowing this feeling is what brings us the greatest joy. You'll feel vulnerable in ways you've never felt before, but it's a price worth paying for your freedom and peace of mind.

You may have blocks you do not know how to move: It goes without saying when we begin to clear out the old and bring in the new, we can expect some resistance. The last thing you may want is a new way of being, even if it's better. I'm speaking about the issue of blocks along your journey. Because it's very difficult to walk your path, we all need help in certain areas of our lives, so opening up to other people who can support us will make a difference as we take on this challenge. No one person has all the answers, and there are no shortcuts when bringing your shadow into the light.

Tip: Each and every one of us has something that needs to be healed, so don't listen to the naysayers who tell you that this process won't work. Something deep inside of you is worth taking care of, even if it means making some changes to your life. The fact that there's a block also means that there's a breakthrough. Just be patient and take it easy on yourself. No one said this was a day's job.

The plan may not be clear enough for you: When we are speaking about how big the shadow can be, it can feel like we're talking about an alien life form we need to discover and understand for us to begin moving forward with our lives. I'm speaking about the issue we all have within ourselves, which can be so hard to grasp when we don't know where to begin. Sometimes it's hard to see the truth, especially considering how deeply it is buried in each of us.

Tip: Your understanding of who you are, and your life experiences may be limited; this doesn't mean you cannot grasp the concept, only that it may take some time. Keep moving forward on your journey and take it one step at a time. Like anything else worth doing with our lives, this takes practice until we get better. Be patient with yourself and keep taking those tiny steps forward.

You can't please everyone: The shadow will never be able to fully disappear until we no longer choose to be a victim, whining about not being enough for someone or something. We are all born with different gifts, and each one of us has a different opinion about the way we live our lives. You may not like certain people, places, or things, and they may not like you back either, but you'll still have to deal with them in this lifetime anyway. At the same time, you may find great satisfaction in knowing that you're here and making a difference in some people's lives by choosing to do this work to be a better version of yourself each day.

Tip: There's only one way to live our lives, and that's with a positive attitude. It's not so important what other people think of us because it's most important that we think of ourselves with love and acceptance.

Benefits of Bringing Your Shadow into the Light

You with will have more clarity: The better we get at seeing our shadows and truly accepting them for who they are, the clearer our lives will become. We all have a choice in this life, and it's up to us to choose whether or not we will learn from each moment as it passes by. We benefit greatly from the knowledge that prepares us for what's next in our lives when we do.

You will find healing: Nothing is impossible when you're ready to heal and allow yourself to be happy again on this planet. True healing can happen when there is a change before everything can progress forward into a better place. We cannot expect someone else to heal us, but we can lay the groundwork for ourselves through self-discovery.

You will naturally attract a better life: All of the people and experiences you need in your life will come to you when you're ready to receive them. Your intuition will guide you where to go and who to be with, so don't put yourself in a position where people and situations that don't suit you'll be able to control your thoughts or emotions.

You will realize that many of your blockages are emotional: The emotional self is difficult to deal with because the human body is filled with energy, which is what runs the show. If we can clear out some of the emotions that are blocking us from taking action and moving forward, then we'll be on our way to better beings who aren't afraid to be vulnerable.

You will feel more empowered as a person: When you're willing to take on this journey, you're permitting yourself to do something that few others can do: work through their emotions to find their true selves. This takes time and will involve an inner conflict, but it's all worth it when you get there.

You'll be able to love yourself: Self-love is the greatest gift we can give to ourselves, especially when we've come this far and done so much work. Love yourself and be proud of who you are and where you've been on your journey thus far. You are an amazing person who is worth every bit of love you may have kept hidden in your heart because it's time to see yourself in a new way that hasn't been possible until now.

You'll have a more positive view of life: The biggest task we can face is learning to accept that every moment brings us new things and opportunities. When we give ourselves permission to see this truth and step outside of our comfort zones, we can see how miraculous life is.

Quiz: Have I Brought My Shadow into the Light?

1. Have I been able to accept myself as I really am?
2. Do I have the courage and strength needed to completely heal my emotional issues?
3. Am I no longer afraid of making "too much progress?"
4. Am I willing to see the shadow in me as an opportunity to obtain clarity?
5. Will I be willing to go through the uncomfortable process of learning to love myself more?
6. Can I accept the idea that life is a miracle, and every hour brings something new?
7. Do I have faith that when I've done everything in my power, the universe will take care of the rest?
8. Am I willing to keep climbing when others nearby are losing their footing so that I can be on the path to success?
9. Am I willing to take this journey by myself and make changes that others can be a part of as well?
10. Am I willing to fight for what I want?

11. Do I have a positive attitude about the future and the path ahead of me?
12. Can I accept that each day brings something new and that each person, place, or thing has something valuable to teach me?
13. Am I confident enough in my abilities to believe that there's no obstacle too great for me?
14. Have people been able to tell me things about myself with no fear of backlash from me?
15. Am I willing to see the truth about who I am and the person that I'm becoming?

Chapter 10: Shadow Work: A Stage of Spiritual Awakening

What Is Spiritual Awakening?

Spiritual awakening is a process where an individual gains profound insight into the true nature of the world and of self. In this process, one gains a sense of universal or cosmic consciousness, which can be described as a feeling of knowing everything and being connected with all things. Spiritual awakening is not simply a shift in thinking but also an intense emotional and physical experience that one may feel at various points in their life. Furthermore, every individual is unique in their own way, so experience varies from person to person.

How Is Shadow Work Essential to Spiritual Awakening?

When we are doing shadow work, we dig deep within ourselves and look at things we have kept hidden from the world by exposing them to light. It can be very difficult to deal with emotions that come to light when we do this. We may feel vulnerable or ashamed at some point during the process. However, that is the purpose of shadow work, and it can ultimately result in a spiritual awakening if you continue to push through self-doubt and shame.

Spiritual awakening is a process that takes time, effort, and commitment. You must keep working on yourself for it to last; otherwise, you may find your old ways creeping back in. Shadow work is a process in which one becomes aware of their weaknesses, negative traits, and imperfections to improve upon them. Shadow work allows one to take a more objective look at themselves and their place within the universe. This process can assist in realizing your true self, gaining personal empowerment, and developing identity.

Shadow work is essential to spiritual awakening because it assists one in watching out for the areas within themselves that are holding back progress in other areas of life. It also allows for a deeper understanding of oneself and personal growth. Ultimately spiritual awakening is about learning to see the entirety of who we are as human beings, and this includes all aspects of ourselves, including our shadow side.

How Shadow Work Exercises Can Cause Spiritual Awakening

Meditation is a shadow work exercise that can help cause spiritual awakening.
https://pixabay.com/images/id-5353620/

Shadow work exercises can cause spiritual awakening by assisting one in looking within themselves. Through this process, one can better understand their shadow self and ultimately learn to accept them for who they are. As we become more accepting of our weaknesses, our negative traits, and imperfections, we will understand that they are just part of the human experience and no longer a burden. Through practicing shadow work exercises, one will learn to love and accept themselves as they are and emerge into self-love.

Shadow work is essential to developing the ability to recognize ourselves within our surroundings. This process allows us to understand that we are not separate from each other or disconnected from the world around us in any way, shape, or form. We are all connected and part of one global consciousness.

Shadow work helps us become aware of our place in the world and cultivate acceptance for everything that is part of ourselves and our experiences on this Earth. This process allows one to hone their personal empowerment to live a life filled with purpose and fulfillment.

To achieve a true spiritual awakening, an individual must be willing to embark on a journey of self-discovery that may sometimes be uncomfortable. As previously stated, the initial phases of shadow work can be stressful and may make you feel vulnerable. However, if you push through these feelings, you'll begin to understand who you are as a person and your place within the universe. When this happens, it can have profound effects on one's self-esteem and sense of identity, which can lead to increased clarity in other areas of life.

It is also important to note that not all exercises will cause a spiritual awakening. Many spiritual awakening exercises, such as meditation and mindfulness practices, are designed to help one become more in tune with themselves. Furthermore, these exercises will leave an individual feeling calm and relaxed and potentially cause a spiritual awakening in the long run but will not necessarily prompt the process.

How Spiritual Awakening Is about Embracing All Aspects of the Self

As individuals become more accepting of the parts of themselves they were previously ashamed of or avoided, they will begin to appreciate and love these parts. Regarding the shadow, one must be willing to accept them for who they truly are to fully embrace them.

Our perspective of ourselves and the world around us is constantly changing. One's perspective on an aspect of themselves may change over time as well; for example, you may think you look fat at one point in your life but then lose weight later on and begin to view yourself as fit rather than fat or gain more weight and look at the past "fat" you as being rather fit. The way we perceive ourselves is not always an accurate reflection of who we are.

In fact, many individuals leave out parts of themselves that they have hidden from others or themselves to live up to societal standards or other expectations they feel they must meet. For example, some avoid their desire to help others and devote their time and energy to making money. Others might be timid or shy but try to mask it by being outgoing and aggressive. By avoiding one's "dark side," we are left feeling incomplete as a person and lacking a sense of self-love. This can be dangerous to one's mental health over time as well. As a result, it is important to accept yourself for who you are and allow others to do the same.

The shadow work process will assist one in facing the aspects of themselves they have been avoiding, to become aware of what they are, and to make peace with them. It will then allow individuals to release the shame or fear from these negative traits, emotions, or experiences to gain self-acceptance. This process can lead to spiritual awakening because once individuals accept themselves for who they are, their sense of identity will be enhanced, and self-esteem will improve.

Signs of Spiritual Awakening

You become aware that there's more to life than you previously realized: You may have thought that your life was pretty mundane in the past. Wake up, go to work, make money, and return home. Try not to step on people's toes, be nice to the neighbor, pay your bills, keep your head down and be a good citizen. However, as you begin to awaken spiritually, you'll discover that there's so much more to you and life than you ever thought possible. You will begin to wonder about your true purpose in the grander scheme of things and how you can make the most out of this life.

You become more aware of your surroundings: It's easy to get caught up in the hustle and bustle of everyday life and take things around you for granted. However, as you develop spiritually, you begin to notice more details about your environment, including other people, plants, animals, and how everything is connected. You'll feel a deeper sense of purpose and meaning in life as you reflect on how fortunate you are to be here at this very moment in time.

You feel a growing sense of empathy: Empathy is truly one of the greatest gifts one can possess for yourself and others around you. As you develop spiritually, you'll find that you're more in tune with the feelings of others and their suffering. You'll want to provide comfort and help ease their pain and suffering because it may remind you of something that happened in your life. Personal experience is a great teacher, so if you can relate to something, then maybe it's worth listening to.

You're no longer identified with your ego: One of the most important things that spiritual awakening teaches us is that we are not our egos. As we awaken spiritually, we begin to realize just how much our egos get in the way of living in the present moment. Not only is this an important lesson, but it's also a great one because when we are living in the present moment, we are also connected with our higher self. When you're not identified with your ego, you'll experience a profound sense of peace and joy because you're no longer living in the past or worrying about how you will get through tomorrow.

You discover the connection between all things: As your understanding of reality increases, your connection to the world around you and everything else in existence. You'll feel a deep sense of gratitude for being alive and for all that this means. Your heart will open up and begin to feel more compassion for all that is around you and for yourself.

You become more aware of your senses: As you awaken, you'll begin to be more in tune with all the different facets of your being and how they vibrate at various frequencies. You'll also become more conscious of how these frequencies can affect the emotions, thoughts, and behaviors of others. You will discover that it's important to allow yourself to be present at this moment as you're experiencing life.

You feel weightless: It's normal for people to feel insecure about their bodies because we tend to compare them with others' looks and build unattainable bodies for us. But as you awaken, you'll realize that you're far more than a physical body, and your thoughts, feelings, and behaviors are just as important as everything else about you.

You feel things more deeply: As we can accept ourselves for who we are, it's possible for us to feel everything that is happening in our lives at a deeper level. The deeper the emotion or feeling we have, the greater our ability to connect on a very personal level. We begin to search for meaning in our lives, and this quest leads us to what we believe is "true." Many have difficulty finding some sort of spirituality because they don't know where it can be found or if it's even real.

Stages of Spiritual Awakening

1. **Noticing spirit:** The first thing that happens is realizing that there is so much more to life than just the physical aspects. At this stage of spiritual awakening, you stop thinking about yourself and what you need to do to survive but start thinking about consciousness on a grand scale. You feel almost like a hero in a movie who has been summoned from their mundane everyday life to a grander adventure than anything they had ever considered for themselves. There comes a time in everyone's life or the moment when things change you forever, and you realize that you cannot simply continue living the way you've always done. You realize the only options are to evolve or die. For some people, this pivotal moment could result from losing a loved one, a terrible breakup of a major relationship, a near-death experience, some grand illness, or losing a cushy job. It doesn't matter what triggers this moment for you, but it will happen if it hasn't already. This experience will trigger you to your core. It will cause you to realize that the way you've always looked at life is no longer appropriate for this aspect of your journey. It will shake you awake. When it does, you can either close your eyes and go back to bed or choose to go on the adventure that the event is summoning you to embark on. At this point, the smart thing to do is to heed the call because if you do not, life will create a new set of circumstances with the same old story to wake you up once more. It's not a pleasant cycle to get stuck in.

2. **Selecting your path:** At this point of your awakening, you come to realize that your worldview must expand, and for that to happen, you must choose a path to go on your adventure. This period is as exciting as it is scary and unfamiliar. Everything you've ever believed about yourself, the people in your life, and the world around you will be questioned, and you will be forced to change your stance on many things. This is the point where some people turn to religion, and others turn to spiritual practices like meditation. Others still would turn to psychedelics to explore their inner consciousness and the world's consciousness. Some will select multiple paths to find the answers they seek. No one should tell you whether or not the path you are on is right for you or not. Let your heart guide you.

3. **Walking the path**: You become a seeker in this phase of your awakening. You study everything you need to know about yourself and the world around you to connect with the true reality of life. The further down the path you go, the more familiar it grows, but also new challenges will present themselves so that you are not completely comfortable. The typical expectation in this phase is that you'll go from using external frames of reference, like what you have and where you are in life, to your internal frames of reference, such as spiritual guidance and deep-seated intuition. When you have problems or challenges, instead of using the old ego-based formats of looking for external solutions, you're likely to just sit down and be still in meditation to find the answers from within. You know you're making progress along your path when you feel lighter and lighter each day, and joy is your regular state of being. You don't care too much about taking life so seriously, and you are no longer easily roped into the melodrama which is regular life for others. Another sign that you are doing well on your journey is when your desires finally come to pass with ease. Where you used to struggle long and hard to make your dreams come true, you now manifest them with ease and flow. Everything you are involved in is influenced by grace. You experience constant miracles and happy little "coincidences" in your life, taking you closer to your ultimate purpose.

4. **Losing your way:** This is another phase of the spiritual journey the sojourner must be aware of. No one said spiritual awakening would always be a bed of roses. On this path, you'll be forced to face your cognitive biases and the many ways you have continued to deceive yourself. You'll need to make peace that you were not perfect and have many shortcomings. The challenge set before you entails being willing to adapt, changing your thoughts and emotions and how you perceive things so that you are full of compassion and understanding. You might also find that certain things outside of you will come to challenge your newfound awakened self, and it is up to you not to give in to the temptation to quit on your journey. At this point, so many people sadly choose to go back to the life they knew before they woke up. If this ever happens to you, don't worry. Rest assured that life will come knocking at your door again to wake you up once more. However, it's much better to keep going rather than start again from scratch. The things that

challenge you may come in the form of your personal beliefs, limiting situations, actual physical enemies, or setbacks on your path. They keep you from getting to a higher ascended level of consciousness. All these are engineered to cause you to doubt yourself. But you must stay true to your path. As the great Robert Frost once said, "The only way out is through."

5. **Becoming one with your path:** This phase of spiritual awakening is transcendence. You realize how connected you are to all of life, and you no longer see the distinction between you and another. You can see God in everything. One may assume that to get to this phase, you need to accumulate a lot of knowledge and experience, but that's not the case at all. As a matter of fact, the way to get to this point is by letting go completely of everything that you think you know. You continue to peel back the layers of ego until there is nothing left other than pure consciousness or awareness, which is known as the state of I Am. No matter what stage of your journey you're on, even if you haven't awoken yet, this is the state that we are all seeking in the end.

Quiz: What Stage of Spiritual Awakening Am I On?

1. Have I recently experienced something that has caused me to question life?
2. Do I get the sense that there might be something more than my everyday routine?
3. Do I feel restlessness and dissatisfaction within me?
4. Am I feeling uncertain about the beliefs I hold about life?
5. Have I come to a point where I am desperate for change?

If you answered yes to at least three out of five of these questions, you are in the first stage of spiritual awakening.

1. Am I currently seeking a path to explore my spirituality?
2. Are there several paths that I have been seriously considering lately?
3. Do I feel a sense of fear mingled with excitement?
4. Is my intuition pointing me towards a specific teacher or spiritual practice?

5. Do I realize that once I begin this journey, I will not look back, and I am at peace with that?

If you answered yes to at least three out of five of these questions, you are on the second stage of your journey.

1. Have I chosen the paths and tools that I desire to use to explore my spiritual side?
2. Am I finding myself learning more and yet, desiring even more knowledge?
3. Am I starting to look within myself for answers instead of trying to control the outside?
4. Would I say that my life is a lot lighter now than before I started the spiritual path?
5. Have I noticed a lot more synchronicity around me?

If you answer yes to at least three out of five of these questions, you are under the third phase.

1. Am I beginning to lose my way on this spiritual path I've chosen?
2. Have I begun to notice just how imperfect I am?
3. Am I dealing with the discomfort of my cognitive biases?
4. Have I noticed a tendency not to be consistent with my practices?
5. Do I sometimes get so frustrated with myself that I want to go back to where I started?

Answering yes to three out of five questions means you are in the fourth phase, where you lose your way if you don't stick with it. Keep going. It's worth it in the end.

1. Have I found it increasingly difficult to judge anyone or anything because I understand they are part of me?
2. Has my thirst for knowledge been replaced by the satisfaction of simply experiencing life?
3. Do I now understand that the ego is not who I am but a tool to be used as needed?
4. Have I finally realized that I am greater than concepts such as success and failure?
5. Do I now understand that there is nothing to do but simply be?

If you answer yes, to at least three of these questions, you are in the final stage of spiritual awakening. Enjoy this, but also understand that awake people may fall asleep. If you ever do fall asleep, it's okay because how can you wake up if you're not asleep, to begin with? Awakening is an ongoing process. Don't ever beat yourself up, no matter what part of the process you find yourself in.

30-Day Guide to Spiritual Awakening through Shadow Work

Day 1: Sit down for fifteen minutes and simply pay attention to your breathing in meditation.

Day 2: Take out your journal and write down all the positive things about yourself that you can think of. Read through your list and contemplate each point for a minute or two when you're done.

Day 3: In your journal, write down all the negative traits you can think of. When you're done, go through the list, and do your best not to judge yourself. Just accept those truths without making a call on whether they're "right" or "wrong."

Day 4: Go back to the entry you made on day 2, and write the opposite of everything you noted as being good about you. When you're done, sit for about ten to fifteen minutes trying to recall times you acted "bad." Don't judge yourself.

Day 5: Do the mirror work exercise from this book.

Day 6: Pick a few affirmations from this book, about two to three, and focus on what they mean to you for just ten minutes. If you get any insights, you may write them in your journal.

Day 7: Think about a challenge you're facing, and then recall the first time in life you ever felt that certain emotion when you faced that issue. Journal about the challenge and the very first memory you have about that emotion.

Day 8: Pick one aspect of yourself that has kept holding you back and write a letter to it.

Day 9: Do the 3-2-1 technique for an aspect of your shadow that you want to address and integrate.

Day 10: Journal every insight you've had so far from your exercises from day one till this point. Note three ways in which you can do better in your day-to-day life.

Day 11: Spend time in a situation or with people that "trigger" you into feeling uncomfortable in some way. When you feel triggered, pay attention to the thoughts and emotions you have and journal them.

Day 12: Revisit everything you wrote down from the previous day, and think about how the attributes that make you uncomfortable about a situation or person are also within you. Think about ways in which you constantly, unconsciously have sought them out. Write down your discoveries.

Day 13: Sit down with your mirror and do five affirmations today. Pick the hardest ones for you to accept, and as you say each one, really mull over what it means to you.

Day 14: For fifteen minutes, sit and contemplate the fact that you aren't perfect. Look over the entry from day 11, and this time, get comfortable with the fact that people think and feel this way about you too.

Day 15: Sit in front of your mirror, and allow times that you've been terrible or done something you're not proud of to come to your mind. Allow each experience to play out fully in your mind's eye, and when you're done, affirm to yourself while looking in the eye, "It's okay. You did the best you knew to do back then."

Day 16: Do the voice dialogue shadow exercise as outlined in this book. Write down your insights.

Day 17: Do the "standing up to your "good' self" exercise as outlined in this book. Write down your insights.

Day 18: Speak with two to three close, trusted people. Let them tell you three to five good things and three to five bad things about yourself. As you listen, pay attention to any impulses you feel within you to disagree. Note down what they say about you. Note what you agree with and what you don't agree with. Sit down and ask yourself "why" on both counts. Write down your insights in your journal.

Day 19: Do the draining versus energizing exercise, and decide to do at least one thing to give yourself more energy and joy in life.

Day 20: Sit in silence, and reflect on everything you've learned from day 11 to this point. Note down any new insights that may come up within you.

Day 21: Do the "speak aloud exercise" in this book, and make sure you record anything you learn about yourself and how your mind works.

Day 22: Write another letter to another aspect of your shadow self you seek to integrate so that you can finally make progress in the aspect of your life that seems to be holding you back.

Day 23: Journal about one or two traumatic experiences from childhood. Find the thread to learn how it affects you right now as an adult. When you've got it, sit down in front of the mirror and repeatedly affirm, "Who I was back then doesn't affect who I am right now. I can choose to be better."

Day 24: Spend some time with those who make you feel good. Pay attention to what you love about them. Then, later on, write down your insights on their behavior. Sit with what you've written, and contemplate the fact that those qualities are within you, too. Notice anything you struggle to accept and follow the emotional thread to find out why. Write down your insights.

Day 25: Pick five affirmations from this book and use them in your mirror work today. Go as long as it is comfortable for you, and make sure you remember to feel the truth of each word; if you sense any blocks or trouble accepting something, journal about why.

Day 26: Do the voice dialogue exercise for another aspect of your shadow you would like to bring back home. Note down any insights you get.

Day 27: Sit in meditation today for just fifteen minutes, allowing yourself to feel nothing but love as you breathe. If you need help conjuring the emotion, think of someone dear to you or a moment in time when you felt nothing but love. As you end the meditation, visualize your shadow self in your mind's eye, and hug it tightly with all the love you feel within.

Day 28: Write a letter to the aspect of you that feels undeserving of love and good things. Contemplate and write about how this aspect of your shadow has tried to protect and help you. Thank it for its services and ask that it release you with love in your heart and true appreciation for why it had to do what it did.

Day 29: Do the rainbow-bright healing tube technique before going to bed. When you wake up in the morning, journal your dreams and see what insight you can gain from them. If you can't see anything just yet, come back to it another time.

Day 30: Contemplate everything you've learned from the start of this 30-day journey to this point, and write down anything that strikes you as profound. You may repeat this guide as needed for the next 30 days.

Part 2: Healing the Inner Child

How You Can Begin to Heal the Wounded Soul Within Using Meditation, Awareness, Journaling, and More

Introduction

"Do we ever really grow up?"

We ponder this question every once in a while, sometimes during a joke or a serious conversation. However, it doesn't matter how old we are or how mature we feel; our inner child is always lurking, hoping to be heard and felt. We want to give you a chance to get acquainted with your inner child with the help of this book.

We understand that some people may not be familiar with the term "inner child." The topic may also be a little sensitive, especially if you have experienced something traumatic your inner child is still suffering from. For this reason, we made sure to take a simple approach and treat this subject with the level of sensitivity it deserves. We didn't want to use complicated terminologies like other books on the market that alienate the reader. We put so much thought into writing this book. We decided to use a more understanding and humane tone than the other available books.

We want the reader to look at their inner child with love and understanding to be able to contain their pain. Your inner child isn't a disease symptom; you can't just take a pill to numb its pain. It is a part of you that requires a different type of healing. This is why we have included hands-on methods and instructions to help you with the healing process. All the methods mentioned in this book have proven multiple times to be successful for all kinds of different people. These instructions are clear and to the point to avoid confusion and make it easy for you to follow them step by step.

"What is an inner child?"

This is the question that brought you here. However, the answer isn't just a simple definition you can easily find on Google. There is more to this question, and we provided a detailed answer without making it too complicated. We will cover everything related to the concept of an inner child to help you learn more about yourself.

When you become aware of your trauma and come face to face with your pain, you will be able to heal and grow. However, you should first discover your inner child and learn to accept it, as this is the only way you can begin the healing process. In this book, we will help you take these steps so you can finally grow and let go of your past wounds.

No one said the healing journey is easy. However, it begins with one single step that will put you in the right direction. By reading this book, you are taking your first steps on the journey of healing so you can let go of the past and grow into the best version of yourself. Take a long deep breath, relax, and be ready to meet your inner child.

Chapter 1: The Inner Child Explained

As children, we couldn't wait to grow up and become adults. We have always believed that adulthood is much more fun. You don't live with your parents anymore; you become financially independent and are in charge of your own decisions. You live life on your own terms and experience the freedom that comes with being a grown-up. However, one day your boss gives you a negative evaluation, or you have a huge fight with your best friend, and suddenly, you are back to your six-year-old self. You just want to cry or throw a tantrum and hope for someone to hold you tight and tell you, "Everything will be ok."

It's important to understand what your inner child is.
https://unsplash.com/photos/Ewfrjh0GvtY

What brought these feelings on? This is most likely your inner child coming out of hiding and trying to tell you something. So, what is an inner child? Where has this term come from?

The Inner Child

Psychiatrist Carl Jung first coined the term inner child. After spending some time working on his inner self and trying to understand the reasons behind his childlike emotions, Jung made this discovery. He realized that another part of our personality impacts our actions and decisions. Jung called it "the inner child" to describe the part inside of us that has not grown up and is still stuck in the childhood stage. Some emotions and memories still haunt us and are played like a movie inside our heads, while there are other happy ones that we fondly reminisce about. All of these memories and experiences, whether good or bad, are stored in the unconscious and create the inner child.

The word child always goes hand in hand with innocence, joy, and a carefree attitude. Although the inner child stores these positive emotions and characteristics, it also stores all the negativity, trauma, and pain you suffered in the hands of those you loved and trusted the most, like your parents or teachers. In fact, our personalities begin to shape from three to five years old. Unfortunately, you don't get over these feelings, and they stay with you, influencing your decisions, relationships, and other aspects of your life.

Because of its name, the term "inner child" is sometimes used lightly. Unlike what some people may believe, this term doesn't mean having childish thoughts or acting like a child. It is an aspect of our personality that exists in our unconscious and can be described as a "subpersonality." Simply put, this is another side of your personality that usually comes out when you face adversity.

When your inner child takes over, you make decisions, have thoughts, and display certain behaviors based on your childhood trauma and your inner child's need to protect you. Your inner child isn't aware that you have grown up and your life has changed. Your unmet needs and repressed emotions show up when you least expect them in the form of anger, rebellion, or fear. You may still hold on to certain thoughts and beliefs engraved in your brain since you were a child, like sex is taboo or boys don't cry.

Your past trauma will make your soul heavy due to all the pain and negativity you carry. Every decision you make is driven by fear and the desire to protect yourself from things that aren't real or no longer impact your life.

Your inner child is a wounded soul that was abused emotionally, physically, or both. Maybe your family was emotionally abusive, or you were bullied as a child at home or school, or you were raised by narcissistic parents who couldn't love you the way every child wants to be loved. Just like your body can be covered with wounds after an accident, so can your soul after a traumatic upbringing. However, unlike physical wounds that heal over time, soul wounds don't heal, and your inner child never grows or develops. The pain you have experienced can grow with you, and if you don't take the necessary steps to heal, you will suffer for the rest of your life.

It is vital for your well-being that you become aware of your inner child. Some people may experience tantrums or angry outbursts like a child and have no idea what triggered these emotions. Learning about your inner child and working on yourself will help you heal and experience spiritual awakening and growth. Uncovering your past experiences and understanding the root of your pain and fears will put you on your road to healing.

Although your inner child is the product of your past experiences, it plays a huge role in shaping your personality as an adult. Instead of letting it shape you into someone angry, hurt, or bitter, you can let it help you move on from your past and forgive yourself and others. You can become a more confident person, knowing who you are and what you want. You can finally get to experience the fun and creative part of your inner child now that it is no longer consumed with negativity.

When you experience healing, a weight will be lifted off your shoulder as your soul heals, your spirit awakens, and you experience spiritual growth. You are no longer controlled by fear or trauma.

According to coach and author Cheryl Richardson, "Inner Child work is essential. It's the essence of growth as a whole person." You won't be able to change and let go of the past holding you back and become the person you have always wanted to be if you don't work on your inner child first. Working on it will help you get over your childhood pain and trauma. You will be able to make decisions based on your adult experience instead of childhood fears.

How Is Your Inner Child Shaped?

As mentioned, your inner child is shaped by all your childhood memories and experiences, the good and the bad. It remembers how happy you were when your dad would pick you up from school and take you and your siblings to your favorite pizza place or how happy your grandpa's smile made you every time you came to visit. These things fill you with love and warmth every time you reminisce over these memories. It also remembers how you were the only one in your class that wasn't invited to a birthday party. Your inner child still remembers your mother's pain when she got the news that your grandma passed away. Every single time a kid at school called you a name or made fun of is still engraved in your memories.

It still remembers how your childhood best friend decided one day they didn't want to be friends because you weren't cool anymore or the time your teacher embarrassed you in front of the whole class. It remembers if a parent was physically, mentally, or emotionally abusive or unavailable. How they made you lose faith in your looks every time they tell you to lose weight or make comments about your body when you eat pizza or a chocolate bar.

You grow up a little and reach the awkward teen years. Your inner child is still there, filled with self-doubt as a result of your upbringing. It is with you during your first job interview, afraid, because it still remembers all the time your parents made you feel like you weren't good enough. It shows up when you and your partner fight; you fear they will abandon you just like your parents did or won't think you are good enough – perhaps like your mom or dad made you feel.

Your inner child is shaped by everything you have ever experienced, seen, heard, and felt. All your positive and negative experiences influence who you are today. Even the smallest things your parents taught you to, like how you should stay in your job even if you hate it or you should put make-up on, or no one will look at you. Simply put, your inner child is shaped by your entire childhood. Even the experiences you may not remember are still living in your unconscious mind, triggering you.

Other childhood experiences that shaped your inner child include:
- Constant abuse by a parent
- Not being allowed to have an opinion

- Your parents, siblings, or other family members constantly shame you
- Your boundaries were constantly violated
- You weren't allowed to be different, and you were even punished for it
- Every time you spoke up, you were yelled at or punished
- Your parents never hugged you or showed you affection
- Your family never allowed you to express your feelings, whether they were positive (like joy) or negative (like anger)
- Your parents made you feel responsible for their happiness
- Your parents didn't allow you to be a child and to play or just have fun

How Your Inner Child Impacts Your Adult Life

Every once in a while, your wounded inner child will take over and start acting out. Your wounded soul is suffering, which can show up as emotional tantrums, outrageous behaviors, or challenges whenever someone tries to get close to you. You also develop certain personality traits as a result of your inner child being stuck in the past.

Serious Trust Issues

This can result from a parent manipulating you or lying to you as a child. You think anyone you let in will hurt you or let you down.

Anxiety

You are always anxious around new situations like going to a new place, meeting new people, or having new experiences. This is mainly because you are uncomfortable with anything or anyone you aren't familiar with and can't predict what will happen or how they will act.

Guilt and Low Self-Esteem

Growing up with parents who blamed you for everything – even things that weren't your fault – can make you feel guilty. Therefore, you grow up as someone who feels like everything is their fault and suffers from unnecessary guilt. When you grow up believing you are always at fault, this can affect your self-esteem, and you never explore your talents or abilities or become aware of your self-worth.

Inability to Set Healthy Boundaries

Saying no and standing up for yourself are examples of setting healthy boundaries. However, suppose your family never respects your boundaries or accepts "no" as a full sentence. In that case, you become a people pleaser and put everyone else above yourself and your happiness.

Fear of Abandonment

You think everyone will leave you like your friends or parents (this can result from being abandoned by a parent as a child). A fear of abandonment can also lead to a fear of commitment. Even if your loved one did everything to prove they would never leave, your inner child would prevent you from believing them.

Difficulty Managing Your Emotions

As a child, you were probably neglected or abandoned by a parent. Instead of blaming them for leaving, you think it is your fault. This makes it difficult for you to manage your emotions and direct your anger to the right person.

Fear of Speaking Up

Maybe your parents judged you every time you spoke up or made you feel unheard or that your opinion didn't matter. This can also prevent you from setting healthy boundaries, and you give others a chance for others to control your life.

Addiction Tendencies

If you are addicted to drugs or alcohol, this can be your inner child trying to numb the pain instead of confronting it. Addiction is one of the most obvious and dangerous signs your inner child needs attention.

You Feel Unloved

Suppose your parents were emotionally unavailable when you were young. In that case, you grow up feeling unloved because no one showed you that you are worthy of love.

Negative Thoughts

Whenever you are upset or face a challenge like not getting a job, you start having negative and belittling thoughts about yourself, such as "I am not good enough" or "I don't have the right skills." Maybe your parents never believed in you as a child or constantly compared you to a sibling.

You Are Easily Triggered

Any situation, whether big or small, can trigger you one way or another because you remember similar situations that took place when you were a child. You spiral out of control, which can affect your well-being, relationships, and career.

You Seek Other People's Approval

If you grew up with parents who never validated you or your feelings, you would constantly seek approval elsewhere. You can't comprehend that validation comes from deep within.

Everything you do is nothing more than a defense mechanism your inner child uses to protect you from further pain.

Spiritual Growth and Mental Well-Being

How can you experience spiritual growth and improve your well-being if your inner child is running the show? The first step towards healing is understanding you're not the one in control. There is another side to your personality in your unconscious mind holding you back to protect you from getting hurt. If you ignore this part of yourself or you pretend that it doesn't exist, just like a child, it will manifest in anger outbursts and tantrums. How do you deal with an angry child? You give them attention and try to understand the source of their pain.

Now that you know your inner child is responsible for some of your negative traits or unpredictable behavior, you can begin a dialogue and start to form a relationship with it. Your inner child is trying to tell you something; it is screaming for help and trying to get your attention. Listening to your inner child will allow you to take a peek into its world and learn about its pain, sufferings, hopes, and needs. This can be achieved through various methods like mediation which we will discuss in detail in the coming chapters.

Once you begin listening to your inner child and navigate through all the trauma, pain, and anger it has been holding on to, you will understand that it requires spiritual healing. Giving your inner child attention is like peeling different layers of yourself. You will begin to learn more about this part of your personality and understand what it needs so you can provide it. You may uncover things about yourself, like repressed memories or emotions.

The more you learn about your inner child, the more you understand what it needs and how to nurture it, meet its needs, and give it the love and attention it has always sought. You will begin working on its healing until it is no longer consumed with the fear that is holding you back. Once your inner child feels safe, you will also notice a difference in yourself and every aspect of your life. You will become more confident, happier, and more comfortable in your own skin. Your inner child will become a voice to motivate you to live the life you have always wanted and experience new things instead of being a voice that prevents you from living your life out of fear.

As a result of nurturing your inner child, you will experience spiritual healing and, thus, spiritual *growth* because you ate longer stuck in the past. Your inner child is now growing and evolving with you. When your spirit heals, your well-being will thrive, and your physical and mental health will improve as well.

Each of us has an inner child trying to communicate with them. Yours is part of who you are, and it is time to give it the attention it deserves. This is the only way you can let go of the past and lead a life filled with love and positivity instead of allowing fear and trauma to take the wheel.

Chapter 2: Archetypes of the Inner Child

Archetypal patterns can be found everywhere. When we understand the importance of learning about them and begin digging deep into their meanings, we can learn a lot more about ourselves and the world around us. Have you ever seen a grown man turn into a child right before your eyes? Maybe their face suddenly lit up, and they started giggling uncontrollably when they heard their favorite song on the radio. Maybe this was the first time you've ever seen them let loose and drop their serious expression. How does this extreme shift happen?

Regardless of how old we get, a child archetype will always live within us. This archetype is born with us and is nurtured throughout our lifetime. It is the stepping stone of our entire personality, growth, and personal development. The greatest thing about the child archetype is that it's so much more than just a mental formulation of the human mind and psyche; it is also an aspect of our souls. Child archetypes are ever-lasting and never diminish, nor are they an invention of our past experiences, as opposed to popular belief.

The child archetype continues to impact our actions, behaviors, and view of life even as adults. The inner child affects our perceptions, understanding of everything around us, and interpretation of the world. The impact of the archetype is typically the most prominent when it comes to concepts of nurturing ourselves, caring for others, family, our outlook on life, loyalty, and safety. Connecting with your inner child requires you to reflect on your unmet desires during your childhood. You must also explore your unhelpful and childish behaviors, particularly those that influence your relationships' quality and your ability to make rational and calculated decisions. Think of your inner child as a child of your own. Your child archetype is your first child. You need to nurture it, care for it, parent it, and continue to raise it throughout your life journey. Nurturing your inner child is perhaps the greatest act of self-care there is. It is the best gift you can ever offer yourself.

There are two sides to the child archetype: the conscious, which is also known as the light side, and the unconscious, which is the dark or shadow side. In other words, the former represents your independence, and the latter corresponds to your dependence. The polarity of the inner child can be essentially thought of as how you handle your responsibilities, balance your duties, depend on yourself or others, and how others can depend on you. Acknowledging your inner child, exploring its needs, catering to its needs, as well as cultivating a healthy relationship with it can allow you to improve these aspects of your being. It can help you unleash your creativity, improve your relationships, heal past traumas, make better decisions, and attain independence.

In this chapter, you will learn more about the inner child archetype and how it can help you promote your spiritual well-being. You will then learn about the six archetypes, find out their attributes and signs, and understand their challenges. Finally, you will come across a quiz that can help you identify the archetype your inner child encompasses.

What Is the Inner Child Archetype?

When we say that the child archetype overtakes someone, we don't necessarily mean that they're acting childish. It's not their behavior that reflects the archetype, for the most part, but rather their repressed thoughts and conversations that go on inside their minds. Your inner child is begging to come out when you can't seem to shake the overwhelming emotions and thoughts tied to your childhood. Your child archetype, at its core, is the part of you that ensures that all your actions are aligned with the first thing it has learned, which is the construct of cause and effect.

Your inner child yearns for safety and protection. It wants a secure, perfect life. It will do everything within its power to ensure that you're protecting and nurturing it. At the same time, your child archetype is convinced that everything, whether good or bad, happens to you because you deserve it. The next time you tell yourself that you don't deserve your friend's betrayal, for instance, know that this is your inner child speaking.

Your child archetype sees life as black or white. It is not yet cognizant of the grays and blurry areas. It will only recognize events as either fair or unfair. It will only view you as either deserving or undeserving. When you expect a raise or a promotion, your inner child acknowledges your hard work and therefore believes it's only fair for you to be compensated.

Did you ever seek anyone's validation? You'd be lying if you said you didn't. Even the most confident individuals need someone to tell them that they're doing a great job from time to time. We all need someone to acknowledge our efforts and express how much they're proud of us. This is because our inner child doesn't recognize the concept of self-approval yet. As kids, our perceptions of ourselves were primarily set by how our parents viewed us. We waited to see if our parents would approve of our actions before we approved of ourselves. Our friends at school determined our self-worth. If we were made fun of, we immediately believed something was wrong with us. If we were part of the group, then we were on the safe side. A child, and the inner child, don't realize that we can approve of ourselves before anyone else does.

We all strive for our own self-approval. This is why it's important to realize that no matter how positive people's opinions are of us, they will never fulfill the unshakeable need to love and accept ourselves. Making a conscious effort with your inner child and embarking on the journey to self-discovery and acceptance will eventually lead you to self-approval. Only then will your need for external validation will falter. You will not reject people's approval- it's against human nature. However, you will not be bound to it.

Inner Child vs. Child Archetype

You must understand your inner child before exploring your child's archetype. The idea of the inner child was first developed in the field of healing therapy and psychology during the 1960s. As more people understood the validity and importance of this concept, its popularity grew significantly over the years. Now, it is not just a very important aspect of psychology and mental health but also a pillar of spiritual healing and well-being.

As we mentioned above, the inner child is the aspect of our psyche that is made of all we experienced and learned throughout our childhood.

Working with this aspect of our spiritual and psychological being will allow you to determine the looming needs and wishes that have never been catered to in your childhood. This journey will also help you uncover immature behaviors and shadow patterns (remember the two sides of the child archetype?) that result in harmful behaviors and destructive life choices in adulthood.

On the other hand, the child archetype is not a product of what you've learned. As you can recall, it is also an element of your soul. This timeless aspect of your being is not past-oriented, even though your childhood influences a portion of it. Healing your inner child requires you to face and overcome past traumas or experiences. However, working with your child archetype encourages you to engage with this part of yourself and explore its light and dark (or shadow) ends of the spectrum.

Inner Child Healing

When we speak of the inner child, the idea that often comes up is that of healing. People who have suffered from traumatic incidents in their childhoods can benefit from healing their inner child. Understanding these parts of themselves and approaching them with compassion can help them revisit the memories that they've been repressing for years. Although it's often painful, the process is incredibly transformative. This healing process also applies to one of the child archetypes known as the wounded child.

The Child Archetype Motivations

When it comes to the child archetype, the main tension arises from the dichotomy that highlights the concepts of dependence and independence. There is constant strife between the need to belong and the desire to stand out. We want to be independent but still want to find a place among others. The health of your child archetype is what determines how you find a balance between those two ends of the spectrum. When working with this aspect of your spirit, you must reflect on your dependence and independence patterns. Are you consistently individualistic and hyper-independent or over-dependent, or are you constantly shifting between both extremities? How do you feel about relying on someone from time to time? Do you bite off more than you can chew and insist that you can juggle numerous responsibilities? Perhaps you avoid all commitments whenever you can.

Take the time to reflect on your relationships and responsibilities. Determine the things and people you are responsible for and those responsible for you. It can be very easy to say that you're responsible for yourself and no one else is. However, don't forget to factor in your boss at work, your doctor, your insurance company, your spouse, etc.; They are all responsible for you in one way or another.

Think about the level of your involvement in your community. How "present" are you in terms of your family? Do you have a family of your own? If not, is there a particular reason stopping you from building one? Do you visit your parents or relatives often? What is your relationship with them? Are you an active member of your community? These questions will teach you more about your child's archetype. Whether you go with the flow or take the initiative, standing up for your needs and desires is among the child archetype's most prominent challenges.

Whenever we're feeling overwhelmed or struggling to snap into the present moment, we must take a break from everything. Put your chores on pause, stop working or studying, and let go of the need to make any effort. Allow yourself to take a break from everything, your thoughts included. Call on your child archetype and invite it to spend time with you. Allow it to show you how to play and spend your time. Detach from all expectations and allow yourself to have fun. Discover what you love to do and drop the to-do list for the time being.

The 6 Child Archetypes

There are numerous child archetypes out there. Each archetype manifests its balance of the light and shadow spectrum. They are all associated with a range of positive and negative qualities. Even though we may reflect the traits of several archetypes throughout our lifetimes, we are portrayed by the one that resonates the most with us.

1. The Magical (or Innocent) Child

The magical child is fascinated by everyone around them and is also an element of fascination for others. They manage to find the silver lining in all situations and trust in the innate goodness of others. Innocent child maintains their strength, wisdom, and courage even in times of disaster. They believe that anything is possible and that all can change for the better. They are carefree and enchanted by the world around them. This archetype is the epitome of a dreamer.

However, their shadow side is that they can easily become cynical, even about the things they used to fantasize about for hours on end. They can go from believing in magic and fairy tales to destroying the dreams of others. The magic child's dark side can lead to depression, and their main challenge is that they can resort to fantasy worlds to escape reality. This may be your child archetype if you struggle with TV, books, substance, or video game addictions. When unbalanced, they lose touch with reality. An innocent child often refuses to take the initiative, which causes them to push people away. Instead of pulling themselves out of a rut, they wait for someone to come along and do it for them.

2. The Orphan Child

The orphan child archetype feels like they don't belong. They are not necessarily orphaned but spiritually, emotionally, or even physically abandoned. Their parents or loved ones may have never catered to this archetype's physical and emotional needs. If you're an orphan child, then chances are you struggle to build strong and healthy relationships with your family. You may also struggle with intense feelings of loneliness.

The orphan child may end up making it their mission to become completely independent on their life journey. They are adamant about learning things on their own, overcoming their fears all by themselves, and avoiding groups of people. The only person they trust is themselves. While independence and the keenness on self-growth and development is an upside, this archetype has a strong shadow aspect. The orphan child archetype incessantly pushes everyone away. They isolate themselves and don't allow anyone in. They compensate for this loneliness and feelings of being unwanted by searching for family in alternative places. Their main challenge is the struggle to find balance when it comes to cultivating and maintaining relationships with others. They need to learn to trust.

3. The Wounded Child

As you can infer from the name, the wounded child carries a great deal of trauma and painful experiences from their childhood. Neglect, abuse, and other impactful situations inevitably influence this archetype's relationships, decisions, and coping mechanisms. The wounded child often feels immense anger and resentment toward their caretakers. In most cases, these individuals will take it upon themselves to aid others who have gone through similar experiences. Your wounded child may come into play to protect you if you've ever encountered trauma as a kid.

This archetype usually endures abusive relationships because their shadow side keeps them stuck in a self-victimizing cycle. They can't help but grieve their situation and pity themselves. They're quick to blame everyone around them for how they are and are always going about how horrible things have turned out for them. The wounded child struggles to overcome negative emotions. They feel like no one understands.

On the other hand, their empathy urges them to jump in at the first opportunity to help others, especially those stuck in patronizing relationships. When balanced, the wounded child archetype is compassionate and forgiving. They can be the reason why someone feels understood. They can even serve as a source of strength for those who need to heal.

The main challenge for this archetype is that they may allow their childhood wounds to impact their adulthood and may struggle to find healthy ways to deal with the trauma.

4. The Nature Child

The nature child cultivates deep connections with everything in nature. They can form indispensable bonds with animals and easily communicate with them. They are rooted in the earth and are drawn to animal spirit guides. While they are clearly empathetic, emotional, and sympathetic, these individuals are also strong and resilient.

When balanced, the natural child archetype loves to connect with the earth. They love to breathe in the crisp air, walk barefoot on sandy beaches, and observe the various hues of nature. However, their shadow side may cause them to take their anger out on everything around them. They may abuse people, animals, plants, and nature. Instead of enjoying nature, they take out their negative emotions on it. They may litter, cut down plants, or express unreasonable hatred toward animals.

5. The Eternal Child

The eternal child wants to stay physically, mentally, and spiritually young. This causes them to avoid responsibilities and commitments. These individuals are on a mission to live life to the fullest. They are characterized by their optimistic, bright, and almost innocent outlook on life.

However, these individuals are very resistant when it comes to taking on adult responsibilities. They are very unreliable and often overstep the boundaries of others. The main challenge here is the struggle to accept that aging is an unavoidable aspect of life. They need to acknowledge their responsibilities and find a balance between staying youthful and leaning into adulthood.

6. The Divine Child

The divine child and the magical child archetypes are very similar. However, the divine child archetype is on a rather prophetic mission. These individuals are innocent and pure, making it hard for adults with this archetype to distinguish themselves. At first glance, you may not realize that you have a divine child inside of you.

The divine child compensates for painful experiences by resorting to spiritual endeavors or places associated with joy and development. They have an inexplicable faith that things will work out for the best. They typically believe in a divine entity.

Their shadow side is characterized by a tendency to allow fear to drive their actions. In doing so, they may hurt others before they are hurt.

Quiz: What Inner Child Archetype Am I?

Answer the following yes or no questions in the "answers" section below. The archetype with the highest number of yes answers is the archetype you belong to.

1. I generally feel safe.
2. I was often neglected as a child.
3. I feel misunderstood by other people.
4. I feel at home when I spend time in nature.
5. I run away from responsibilities.
6. I'm always excited about what's to come next.
7. I truly believe that no one intends to hurt another person.
8. Life is a constant series of heartaches.
9. Changes in the world around me scare me.
10. I feel attuned to the natural cycles of the world.
11. I am struggling to find the right job for my needs.
12. I am open to experiencing the adventures of life.
13. I trust that others will take care of me.
14. I am afraid of those in authoritarian positions.
15. I struggle with self-worth and self-esteem.

16. I am afraid of not surviving.
17. I am sometimes overtaken by a false sense of arrogance.
18. I usually find myself the center of attention.
19. I believe that the world is a safe place to be.
20. I feel abandoned.
21. I feel anxious when my sense of security is slightly shaken.
22. I often worry about being betrayed.
23. I try my best to live my life to the fullest, regardless of the consequences.
24. I have faith that things will work out for the best, even when it doesn't seem like it at times.

Answers:

The Innocent Child:

1:

7:

13:

19:

The Orphan Child:

2:

8:

14:

20:

The Wounded Child:

3:

9:

15:

21:

The Nature Child:

4:

10:

16:

22:

The Eternal Child:

5:

11:

17:

23:

The Divine Child:

6:

12:

18:

24:

No matter how hard we try to fight it, our inner child survives within us, demanding its rights. It is an active part of who we are, asking for attention and requiring acknowledgment. The child archetype wishes to be heard. It is where our random playful outbursts, moments of innocence, creativity, and wild imagination come from. While it never goes away, the inner child's voice becomes quieter as we go into our teenage years. With the pressures and expectations that come with adulthood, we often feel the urge to repress the inner child. As this voice grows less prominent, we think we've successfully overcome it, and we think that we can put it behind us forever. However, this is never the case.

Chapter 3: Discovering Your Inner Child

If you don't go back to save your inner child, who will? You are the only one who can connect with it and understand what it is going through. As we grow older, we lose touch with our inner child. We forget about this innocent part of ourselves that still experiences child-like emotions and needs mothering. We neglect our hopes, dreams, and needs and become only concerned with what our adult self wants. Your inner child is also the part that holds on to your pain and trauma, which can impact your decisions and reactions. No one can deny its role in shaping our personality, which begs the question, why don't we pay attention to it?

There is always a hidden reason or a trigger behind our unpredictable actions or reactions. Your inner child is a part of your subconsciousness, holding the answer to the question, "why am I like this?" If you don't acknowledge this side of your personality, you may never fully understand who you are or why you experience certain emotions.

You need to reflect to discover your inner child.
https://unsplash.com/photos/bbjmFMdWYfw

Finding your inner child is vital to your healing. Your wounded soul requires tending to – so you can move on from all the trauma you have experienced through the years. However, how can you fix a problem if you aren't conscious of it? How can you meet your inner child's needs when you don't know what these needs are? Healing requires you to go on a journey of self-discovery and to come face to face with your trauma, pain, and fears. Simply put, to heal, you must confront your inner child to get to the root of your trauma. If you are unconscious of your inner child, it will take over when you least expect it and overpower you.

Discovering your inner child, as the name suggests, is becoming conscious of your wounded soul, recognizing it, acknowledging its existence, and giving it the love and compassion it has always needed. This journey of self-discovery will allow you to embrace and accept your inner child as a part of who you are rather than fighting it, ignoring it, or numbing the pain. That said, you can't go on this journey without first learning to love and value yourself. Believing in yourself, your abilities, and your skills will motivate you to not only discover yourself but also believe that you have it in you to heal your wounds.

As you begin to discover and embrace your wounded soul, you will see this part of yourself as a helpless little child needing love, compassion, and acceptance. Although finding your inner child is greatly beneficial to your wellbeing, it can be a big and terrifying step for some people. You don't know what you will uncover on this journey. Your inner child can be happy and healthy or traumatized by things you may not even remember.

Benefits of Discovering Your Inner Child

Uncovering your inner child will help you release the pain and trauma that wounded your soul. When your inner child is healed, you begin navigating life as an adult who makes decisions and faces challenges instead of being just scared. Our inner child has needs, but every time it communicates them to us, we dismiss them as unnecessary. Needs like love, security, boundaries, spontaneity, and validation are valid needs. If they aren't met, this can affect our mental health. Because of this, you should find your inner child, listen to it, nurture it, and meet its needs to lead a fulfilled and happy life.

There are many benefits to discovering your inner child and connecting with it. Your inner child is trying to reach out to you, and it has been trying to get your attention. So, answer the call, get in touch with this part of yourself, and notice how various areas of your life will improve.

Boosting Your Self-Confidence

Once you get in touch with your inner child, you will begin your journey toward self-healing. Accessing this part of yourself will awaken the playful side of your inner child, who loves to have fun, try new things, and go on adventures. As a result, you will become bolder, more confident, and more determined to achieve your goals. You will have a mentality of "if I can discover my inner child and work on it, I can do anything."

Self-Care

Getting to know your inner child is a form of self-care in itself. It will give you a chance to learn about its needs so you can work on fulfilling them and thus take care of yourself and your wellbeing. Your wounded soul will feel like a real child that you have to care for and protect, like a mother who won't let anyone hurt her baby. Therefore, you will make self-care a priority.

Feeling Playful

As you gain access to your inner child, you learn about the pain, trauma, and fun and child-like aspects of your personality. You free yourself from all the constraints of adulthood, let go, and have fun. You experience a feeling of relaxation away from the seriousness and responsibilities of adulthood, even if it is just for a short while. This can do wonders for your physical and mental health.

Understanding Yourself

Discovering your inner child will reacquaint you with yourself. You will find out things about your past or your personality that you have either forgotten about or repressed, like certain emotions and memories. Through this self-discovery, you can find the source of your pain affecting your actions and decisions as an adult so you can take the necessary steps to work on yourself.

Improving Your Physical Health

Many people aren't aware of the benefits of understanding and getting to know themselves better. Self-awareness helps you relate to others and feel connected to the world around you, making you feel that you belong somewhere. A sense of belonging and community can boost your immune system and improve your physical health.

Self-Love

Self-love is often confused with narcissism or ego; however, it can't be more different. Many people are reluctant to love themselves and consider the whole notion to be strange. Getting in touch with your inner child will make you see yourself in a different light. You get acquainted with this innocent and vulnerable part of yourself that needs to be loved. You will sympathize with it and provide it with the love and compassion it has always yearned for. Once you accept your inner child as a part of who you are, you will experience true self-love.

Symptoms of Discovering Your Inner Child

As you begin your journey of self-discovery, you should be prepared for anything. By accessing this part of your personality, you will experience a wide range of emotions; some are positive, while others are negative. Take advantage of all the positive emotions and let them be a force that drives you to heal, grow, and enjoy life. Negative emotions will give you an idea of the wounds and trauma you have been suffering from all this time so you can work through your issues and finally heal.

Positive Emotions
- Creativity
- Joy

- Playfulness
- A desire to have fun
- A light-hearted attitude
- Feeling less emotionally numb and disconnected

Negative Emotions
- Becoming aware of repressed memories and emotions
- Childhood trauma
- Pain and fear

Challenges of Discovering Your Wounded Soul

Don't expect this journey of self-discovery to be a smooth ride; there will be some challenges along the way you should be prepared for. Connecting with your inner child can be triggering if you have suffered from traumatic experiences during your childhood. You will find yourself being confronted with repressed memories and emotions that you aren't ready to revisit. Remembering things you have fought hard to forget or repress may discourage you from continuing on this journey. It can be challenging to face these memories, so you would rather ignore your inner child than try to uncover your trauma. You may also be ashamed of having a scared and vulnerable inner child. However, you aren't alone; each one of us has an inner child. The only difference is some are happy and satisfied while others are traumatized and struggling.

Many people face these challenges, and it is pretty normal. The pain and fear they experience after being exposed to emotions and memories they have long tried to avoid can be emotionally and mentally draining. As a result, they quit, leaving their inner child wounded and numbing the pain with unhealthy coping mechanisms like alcohol or drugs.

No one said healing is easy, but it is worth it. Learning there is a part of you that is traumatized can be both shocking and hard to deal with. However, you should let this pain motivate you to take your inner child by the hand and help it move on and grow. Once it does, you can be free from past pain. It is a long, hard road that begins with one vital step: discovering your wounded soul.

A Guide to Discovering Your Inner Child

In this part of the chapter, we will provide you with a simple guide to help you uncover your inner wounded soul. Reaching out to your inner child isn't easy. It has its challenges and may take a while. You shouldn't fret or give in; eventually, you will get there and uncover its secrets.

Open Your Mind

Before you embark on your journey of self-discovery, you should first open yourself up to the idea of an inner child. Having doubts at first is normal, but you should regard your inner child as a part of you, not as something separate. Simply put, change your perspective. You aren't discovering your "inner child" per se, but you are discovering your past relationships and experiences. Not believing in the idea of an inner child or that you can connect with it can create a barrier that prevents you from uncovering it.

Daydream

Sit alone in a quiet room, close your eyes, and allow your mind to travel back to your childhood. Think of how simple things were back then with no responsibilities, running free, and being spontaneous and silly. You didn't care about money; the simplest things made you happy. You laughed until your stomach hurt, and the word "stress" didn't even have meaning to you. Now, open your eyes and write down everything you saw and felt. Did these thoughts evoke happy and joyful emotions? Or was your childhood so traumatic that it evoked pain and fear? Write it all down, including what specifically made you happy as a child and what caused you the most pain and suffering.

Do Things You Enjoyed as a Child

Treat your inner child as someone you want to get to know. Try to find what they like so you can connect with them and get close to them. So how can you learn about your inner child's hobbies? Simply think of the things you used to enjoy as a child-like riding your bicycle, swimming in the pool with your best friends, going roller skating, dancing, or spending the day at the library. Whatever you did as a child, you did it for one purpose only: to have fun. You didn't have responsibilities and did things because you wanted to, not because you had to.

Do things you enjoyed as a child.
https://www.pexels.com/photo/photograph-of-two-girls-on-a-swing-1814433/

When was the last time you did anything just for fun? This is the perfect time to do something that used to make you happy. Go back to the time when life was simple with no stress, and your only concern was having fun. Try something creative like coloring, doodling, painting, or playing your favorite video game from your childhood. These activities will relax you, shut down your mind, and awaken emotions you may have forgotten about. Some of these emotions or memories can manifest in your drawings or doodling.

Seek the Help of a Child

As an adult, you may struggle to see things from a child's perspective. Many of us have forgotten how to have a child-like attitude. Seeking the help of a child, like your son, daughter, nieces, or nephews, can be very helpful. In fact, there are many things we can learn from children. Spend some time with any children in your family and play fun games like hide-and-seek or tag. These games will help you let go of the constraints of adulthood as you run around feeling free and having fun. Watching your favorite cartoon as a child or reading your favorite childhood book can bring back positive memories and emotions as well.

You can also try playing make-believe scenarios like pretending you are Darth Vader and running around chasing the kids. Make-believe scenarios can take you back to your childhood fantasies and dreams. However, this game may not always awaken heart-warming emotions and memories. If you experienced trauma as a child and used your imagination as a coping mechanism to escape your harsh reality, you may find yourself remembering these moments.

Start a Dialogue with Your Inner Child

Having a conversation with someone can teach us so much about them. The same can be applied to your inner child as well. We aren't saying you should start talking to yourself (however, if it can help, do it), but you can talk to your inner child through journaling. For instance, if you experienced a traumatic event as a child, writing about it can help you get in touch with your inner child. You can write a letter to yourself or explore some of your memories and write about them in your diary. While writing, think of a specific memory and write everything that comes to mind, don't hold back. You can also do a Q&A by asking your inner child questions and writing down the answers. Acknowledging your inner child at this very moment, embracing the idea without any doubts, and listening to what it is trying to tell you are all crucial for this step to work.

Look inward, self-reflect, and try to access all your buried emotions and memories so you can communicate with your wounded soul. You will not only learn so much about your inner child through writing, but you will also establish a bond with it as well.

Take a Trip Down Memory Lane

Your inner child is still stuck in the past, so you should take a trip back in time to connect with it. You can relive memories in various ways, like looking at old pictures, reading your childhood diary, or looking at your childhood stuff like your toys. Scents are also known to help conjure memories, so try smelling an old perfume or deodorant. For instance, if you catch the scent of your favorite dish, you will remember all the times your grandma made it and all the sweet memories you shared. You can also ask your childhood friends, siblings, parents, or other family members to share stories from your childhood with you. These stories may evoke sweet, bittersweet, or painful memories and emotions.

Seek the Help of a Therapist

This process isn't easy, and you may encounter some challenges along the way. In some cases, trying to uncover your inner child may trigger painful memories and emotions. For this reason, seeking the help of a professional can be what you need to find your inner child. A therapist will walk you through the process of discovering your wounded soul and provide advice and guidance to help you cope with traumatic memories. They can also help you uncover repressed memories and emotions that you buried deep because you don't want to face them. Make sure to find a therapist who has experience in inner child work.

Quiz

We recommend you work on the steps mentioned above for some time first before taking this quiz.

Have I Discovered My Inner Child?

We will provide you with a list of yes or no questions, and your answers will determine if you have discovered your inner child or not. Think hard and take your time with each question.

1. Do you feel more creative than before?
   - Yes
   - No
2. Do you feel more playful and feel like you want to have fun?
   - Yes
   - No
3. Do you feel more in touch with child-like emotions like joy and a carefree attitude or anger and throwing tantrums?
   - Yes
   - No
4. Do you feel the desire to practice an old childhood activity or play an old childhood game?
   - Yes
   - No
5. Do you feel less emotionally numb than before?
   - Yes
   - No
6. Have you recently uncovered a childhood trauma or a painful memory you haven't thought of in years?
   - Yes
   - No
7. Have repressed emotions begun to resurface?
   - Yes
   - No

8. Do pictures or certain scents bring back memories from your childhood (good or bad)?
    - Yes
    - No
9. Do you often daydream about your childhood?
    - Yes
    - No
10. Do you enjoy spending time with children?
    - Yes
    - No
11. Does journaling help you uncover things about yourself?
    - Yes
    - No

Ideally, you should answer "yes" to all or most of these questions. However, if most of your answers are "no," then you still need to work on yourself to discover your inner child.

Don't feel discouraged if you haven't uncovered your wounded soul yet. This is a long process, and it will take time and effort to get there. It can also be a traumatic experience for some people, which can prolong the process.

The road to healing begins with one single step, and this step is discovering your inner child so you can connect with it. It is a road that may be filled with challenges for some people. Your inner child needs you and has been calling out for you through certain child-like actions and emotions. You have been ignoring it for long enough. It is time to act now and give it the attention it needs.

Discovering your inner child will help you learn about yourself and eventually accept the fact that it is a part of who you are. Your wounded soul is a part of your journey, an important chapter in your story that you can't simply ignore or skip.

Chapter 4: Accepting Your Inner Child

"Yes, I feel you, I know you are here, and I accept you."

We all want to be loved, embraced, and accepted for who we are. Our inner child is no different; it yearns for acceptance too. No one can deny the importance of self-acceptance and its role in boosting our self-esteem and leading a healthy and fulfilled life. We all want to be happy; it is the goal most of us chase and has in common. Accepting your inner child will reconnect you with the part of yourself you have been ignoring for so long. You will learn about it, understand its pain, and eventually grow to love it and accept it. Everything you experienced as a child - even the trauma - is part of you and impacts shaping the person you have become. Fighting your pain will only give it power. However, once you accept it as a part of your journey, you take its power away and begin to see your inner child as someone vulnerable, scared, and who just wants to be embraced.

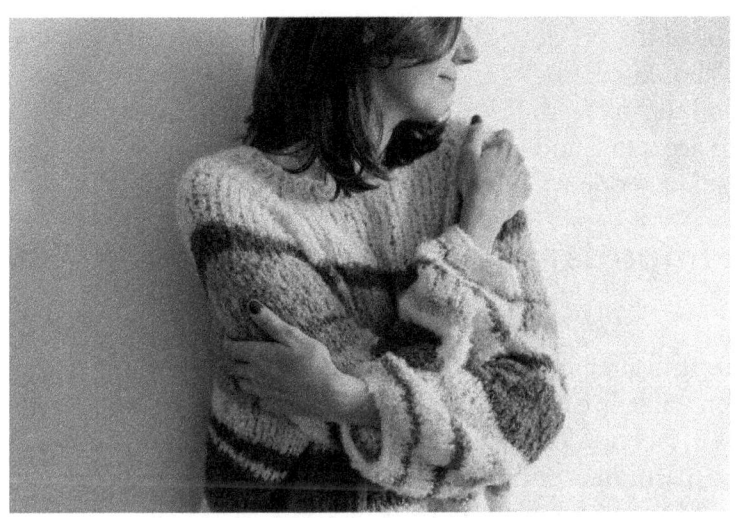

It's important to embrace your inner child.
https://www.pexels.com/photo/a-woman-in-knit-sweater-hugging-self-5709914/

As adults, people usually think they have figured everything out about themselves and the world around them. What if we told you that you not only don't have everything figured out, but you also need to unlearn some of the habits you have picked up over the years? Embracing your inner child is your chance to unlearn all the bad habits and personality traits that resulted from your trauma.

By growing up deprived of love and believing you aren't good enough, your inner child begins seeking perfection and makes you believe that if you aren't perfect, you aren't worthy of love. Perfection is an illusion; the more you chase it, the more frustrated you will be. Eventually, you will despise this part of yourself. However, when you listen, accept, and nurture your inner child, you will understand that it only wants to protect you. Therefore, you stop resenting it and begin to love and sympathize with this vulnerable inner child that doesn't know any better.

Accepting your inner child is just as the name suggests; you fully accept your inner child as part of your past, present, and future and its role in shaping your adult personality. You accept it without judgment or shame and embrace it with all its trauma and pain. Acceptance is the most valuable gift you can give anyone so imagine doing the same for yourself. It is another vital step you should be taking towards healing your inner child and moving on from the past to a brighter and happier future.

That said, you won't be able to accept your inner child before it is fully and truly discovered. How can you accept something you can't find? As mentioned in the previous chapter, discovering your inner child is the first step you should take before you begin your healing. Once you find it and understand that its pain, fear, joy, and trauma are part of who you are, you can begin accepting and embracing it. Your inner child is you; this is a fact you should never deny, fight, or be ashamed of.

The Importance of Accepting Your Wounded Soul

If you are struggling to accept your wounded soul, how will you be able to heal? You can't live your life fighting with a part of yourself or living in shame of it. Acknowledge it and accept it so you can grow stronger and let go of the past. Accepting your wounded soul can help you become a happier and more forgiving person, not just to yourself but to others as well.

Deep inside you lies all the answers you seek. All you need to do is self-reflect, and you will find what you are looking for. You can't keep ignoring your wounded soul. It has been sending you messages all your life through your anxiety, self-criticism, and even depression. Once you fully accept your inner child, you can finally understand the meaning behind these messages. There is a reason behind your anxieties, there is a reason why you want to please people and struggle with saying no, and there is a reason why you have had relationship issues all your life. Your traumatic childhood is the reason behind many of the issues you have in your adult life. Embracing your inner child means you understand that it can be the root cause of many of the problems you have now. You are willing to look for solutions to help yourself instead of silencing or rejecting them.

Accepting your wounded soul means you are ready to heal and are taking the necessary steps to help yourself recover from your past experiences. Your inner child is a sensitive and innocent soul; embracing it means tapping into its positive side with all its wonderful qualities as well. It will remind you to love, forgive, and be honest with yourself and the world around you.

Forgiveness

Kids don't hold grudges. Remember when you were a kid and fought with your best friend or siblings? Did you hold grudges? Kids get over fighting quickly and go back to playing with each other as if nothing happened. When you embrace your inner child, you embrace every part of it, including the ability to forgive. Accepting your inner child will help you see that you are a victim of a bad childhood or bad circumstances. As a result, you will learn to be kinder to yourself and to forgive yourself for any mistakes you have made when your wounded soul takes over.

Honesty

Who is more honest than a child? At times, they can be brutally honest. They speak their mind with no fear of judgment. Unlike us, they don't tiptoe around the truth. When was the last time you spoke your mind without worrying if others would judge you? Do you sometimes hold back from telling the truth? Embracing your inner child will help you approach your relationships and life with an honest attitude. Understanding and accepting that a part of you is damaged will open your eyes and encourage you to be more honest with yourself about your struggles and understand that healing is more of a necessity than an option.

How to Accept Your Inner Child

Now, let's discuss methods to help you accept your wounded soul. We can't stress the importance of embracing this part of yourself enough. In fact, it is an essential step in your healing process.

1. Mother Your Inner Child

Every child needs a mother to nurture and care for them. Embrace your inner child by giving it the motherly love and affection it has always craved. Not every child grows up in a loving home with caring parents. There are narcissistic or immature parents who are unable to love their children. Even the best parents had moments when they were too busy, lost their temper, or yelled at their kids. They never meant to hurt their children, but they are still humans who make mistakes sometimes. However, a child doesn't see it this way, and these things can last with them forever.

As an adult who wasn't loved or is still reeling from certain childhood issues, you are always hard on yourself whenever you make a mistake. You become self-critical, feel guilty, or belittle yourself. Imagine if you treated a child the same way every time they made a mistake. Can you look an innocent child in the eye and belittle them if they do something wrong? How will this affect their mental health and wellbeing? Your inner child, as mentioned, is the child-like part of you, and you should treat it as such. To accept and embrace it, watch your thoughts every time you make a mistake. Instead of the negativity, mother and nurture your inner child by comforting it. Your wounded soul is scared and needs reassurance. Being kind and loving to this vulnerable part of yourself is how you prove that you have fully accepted it.

2. Achieve Your Inner Child Dreams

Think of a dream you wanted to achieve when you grow up. There are no limits to a child's imagination; they believe they can do anything and achieve anything. However, as we grow up, we start having more realistic or practical dreams. Some people in our lives will always discourage us from following our dreams and tell us to look for more steady careers. We forget about these dreams with age, but our inner child still remembers each one we have ever had.

To fully accept this part of your personality, you can achieve one or more of your childhood dreams. We aren't saying you should quit your job or leave your responsibilities behind. You can still achieve your dream without jeopardizing your career. For instance, if you have always wanted to be an artist, you can take an art class, or if you have wanted to be a writer, you can take a creative writing class. Believe in yourself and show your inner child that you still believe anything is possible.

3. Play Games or Dance

We have mentioned in the previous chapter how playing with children, doing something creative you enjoyed as a child, or just dancing can help you discover your inner child. These fun childhood activities can also help you accept your wounded soul. Doing things your inner child enjoys is a great way to show it and to show yourself that you accept and embrace this part of yourself. So, draw, paint, play games, play some music, and dance like no one is watching, or go to karaoke with your friends and sing your heart out. Even if you have a bad voice, don't be afraid of making a fool out of yourself.

4. Listen to Your Inner Child

How can you accept your wounded soul if you aren't actively listening to it? We have talked before about how your inner child communicates with you through strong emotions resulting from triggering situations. Instead of dismissing these emotions, take a closer look at them to understand why you were even triggered in the first place.

For instance, you and your best friend were supposed to meet but canceled at the last minute. Instead of understanding that we all have responsibilities and things can come up, you feel rejected. You act like a child and refuse to answer your friend's calls or messages. When you cool down and see your friend's messages, you realize that their partner had an accident which is why they had to cancel on you. Now you feel terrible for reacting like a "child" and frustrated and angry with yourself.

This tantrum is your wounded soul communicating its pain to you. To show your inner child acceptance, listen to what it is trying to tell you. Understand why it acted this way. Why did you feel rejected when your friend canceled? Maybe your parents were always busy and had to cancel plans or never showed up for your football games or ballet recitals. Listening to your inner child's emotions and seeing the situation from their perspective is a great step toward accepting this part of yourself rather than feeling guilty or rejecting these feelings.

5. Identify Your Inner Child

In a previous chapter, we discussed the archetypes of the inner child and how you can identify yours. Identifying your inner child will help you accept it for what it is without trying to change it.

6. Take Your Inner Child Seriously

You may think whatever your inner child feels is irrelevant to you. Throwing tantrums, feeling rejected, or wanting to play may seem like childish needs to an adult. So instead of paying attention to them, you end up ignoring them. However, there is always a reason behind all your childhood needs, and it comes from something deeper. So, take your inner child seriously and meet its needs.

7. Be Kind to Your Inner Child

Your inner child is hurt, broken, scared, and looking for acceptance. Most wounded souls just want to know they are cared for. No one but you can save your inner child. Remind your hurt and broken soul every once in a while that you love it. Whenever you look in the mirror, say "I love you" to yourself.

If you had a traumatic childhood or were abused or abandoned, your inner child probably believes it was their fault. Now, as you have grown up and realized that none of it was your fault, let your inner child know this as well. Tell it that you didn't deserve this childhood; you deserved to be loved and taken care of.

Apologize to your inner child for how you acted like a child. Whether you were hard on yourself, self-critical, or put yourself last, all these things that you still do to this day are hurting your inner child. Tell your wounded soul you are sorry and protect it from further pain.

We have mentioned in previous chapters that your inner child is driven by fear, and it only wants to protect you. Even though it held you back and stored painful memories, you should still thank it for being there for you and trying to shield you from more pain. Let it know that you aren't judging it and want to thank it for trying.

Accepting your inner child isn't just saying, "I accept you." It is telling it everything it needs to hear so it can heal.

8. Protect Your Inner Child

We have mentioned above how you should treat your inner child like a mother who will protect her baby and won't let anyone hurt it. Your inner child is your baby, and part of accepting it is constantly acknowledging its existence. This is done by checking on it to ensure it is well and keeping it away from harmful situations. Your inner child hasn't healed yet, so show it kindness by respecting its needs. Understandably, you want to let go of your fears and not be held back by them. However, your inner child may have certain insecurities or fears, so treat them more sensitively. For instance, avoid places like elevators if you fear closed spaces - something that began in your childhood. If you have a toxic friend or family member that increases your anxiety, avoid them as much as you can and limit communication with them. Protect your inner child as you protect your real child or your pet.

Accepting Your Inner Child and Spiritual Growth

Accepting your inner child is a process of spiritual growth. It is a long road that will take time and effort. This process isn't just saying to yourself, "I accept my inner child," and then moving on. You must work on embracing and accepting this part of yourself daily. It is the only way you can experience spiritual growth and healing. Take your time with this process and listen to your wounded soul's needs, take these needs seriously, and fiercely protect it just like a mother would.

As mentioned, accepting your inner child is the most important step toward healing. Through it, you will experience real growth. Let your inner child know that you accept it and will no longer ignore it, silence it, or fight it. This is the biggest decision you will make to help accelerate your healing. You aren't only acknowledging your inner child but fully accepting, embracing it, and treating it with the compassion it deserves. You understand that when your inner child heals, you will also heal and experience spiritual growth.

Quiz

Have you fully accepted your inner child? Take this quiz to find out.

1. Have you acknowledged your inner child?
   - Yes
   - No
2. Have you made your peace with the idea of having a traumatized inner child?
   - Yes
   - No
3. Do you feel proud of your inner child for putting up with so much?
   - Yes
   - No
4. Do you love your inner child?
   - Yes
   - No
5. Do you feel grateful for all that your inner child did to protect you?
   - Yes
   - No
6. Do you believe your traumatic childhood was out of your control and not your fault?
   - Yes
   - No
7. Do you feel the need to apologize to your inner child for everything it had to endure?
   - Yes
   - No

8. Do you believe your inner child deserved a better childhood?
   - ○ Yes
   - ○ No
9. Do you take your inner child's needs seriously?
   - ○ Yes
   - ○ No
10. Do you play games or do other fun activities from your childhood?
    - ○ Yes
    - ○ No
11. Are you aware of your inner child's archetype?
    - ○ Yes
    - ○ No
12. Have you tried achieving any of your childhood dreams recently?
    - ○ Yes
    - ○ No
13. Do you believe you have an inner child?
    - ○ Yes
    - ○ No
14. Do you believe your inner child is a part of you and needs healing?
    - ○ Yes
    - ○ No
15. Do you accept having a traumatized inner child?
    - ○ Yes
    - ○ No

If you answer most of these questions with "yes," then you have fully accepted your inner child. However, if you mostly answer with "no," you still need time and effort, but you will get there.

Accepting your inner child is your way of telling your past "no more." You are now taking control of your trauma, and instead of letting it defeat you, you will work on yourself to defeat it and begin your healing journey. Remember, you aren't just healing from your past but also protecting yourself from current or future trauma. Accept your inner child, love it, take care of it, and protect it from pain. When it is healed, it will be the one taking care of you and helping you grow.

Chapter 5: Inner Child Meditation

When you follow the tips from the previous chapters, successfully uncover your inner child, and accept them for who they are, you will see that they have a lot to say. However, having them buried for so long, you may not be able to communicate with your inner child right after acknowledging their existence. This chapter is dedicated to one of the simplest techniques that can help you establish a meaningful connection with your inner self - meditation. You will learn about the impact that practicing meditation has on healing the wounded soul and keeping your mental, spiritual, and physical health in check. After all, these three areas of your life are essential for your inner child's health and happiness - and meditation can help improve all of them. You will also be provided with a beginner-friendly meditation technique you can practice anytime you need to communicate with your inner child or heal yourself.

Meditation plays an important role in healing your inner child.
https://pixabay.com/es/photos/yoga-mujer-lago-al-aire-libre-2176668/

Meditation for Healing a Wounded Soul

The first step in healing your inner child and your soul from within is listening to what they say. This can be challenging as you may have trouble interpreting their messages or simply because you don't like what they are trying to say. The feelings your inner child may convey can trigger powerful emotions and discomfort, which you will only be able to process with the right tools. Not only that, but hurtful feelings such as anger, insecurity, vulnerability, anxiety, guilt, shame, or the feeling of abandonment and rejection can often be traced back to specific memories from your own childhood. Your inner child's feelings are just the reflection of these events - but their discomfort often triggers negative responses in your current life. Meditation is an immersive exercise. It lets you dive deep into the depths of your soul and reveal the origins of the negative thought processes you have in the present time. The root of your spiritual imbalance lies in your inner child's inability to process pain and hurt from the past - and meditative practice can help you move on from these traumatic experiences. To understand how this can be done, you must learn what meditation is and how it works in the first place.

What Is Meditation?

Meditation typically encompasses a range of techniques designed to help you look beyond your conscious thoughts and emotions and uncover what lies within your unconscious mind. By simply focusing your mind into its depths, meditation encourages forming a powerful connection with your inner self, allowing you to experience life more profoundly. Meditation often includes training your mind and body to stay grounded and open to anything you may experience in the present moment.

Meditation and Mindfulness

While meditation is also considered a form of mindfulness, not all mindfulness exercises are as reflective as meditation. Mindfulness brings you to the present - which is the first step in connecting with your inner child and healing them. Whereas meditation is necessary to surpass your conscious mental processes and truly see what the child within you is experiencing. Consequently, if you want to heal your inner child, you must combine these two practices.

Fortunately, mindful meditation is one of the simplest forms of meditation. You can perform it anytime, anywhere. You only need to find a place where you can focus on your thoughts, feelings, and actions as you experience them in the present. You must avoid letting the past or future color your perception, and you shouldn't allow any judgment or preconception to influence you during the process. A mindful meditation focused on healing you from the inside brings your inner child into focus by relaxing your body and allowing your mind to create a specific mental image. Since you have to focus on visualizing the child representing your deepest emotions, you are forced to remain in the present.

Benefits of Meditation for Healing Wounded Souls

As established earlier in this book, your inner child is the reflection of your soul - a reflection that is full of joy and happiness in its natural state. Any negativity your inner child experiences represents your inability to process emotional trauma. Meditation can help you restore the blissful state of your soul by making you aware of all the hurt inside of it. When you are unaware of your soul, you can only focus on your body and mind and the pain inside. However, spiritual imbalances often manifest as physical and mental symptoms, including pain and cognitive issues. By only eliminating the proximate cause of the symptoms, you are only diminishing them- but their true source remains and will eventually cause them to return. You can't comprehend why this is and continue to search for answers - when, in fact, the answers lie right there, within your inner child.

The different meditation exercises can achieve physical relaxation, mental clarity, spiritual connections, and emotional tranquility. All of these have a positive impact on healing your wounded soul and forming a solid bond with your inner child.

Here are the key benefits of inner child meditations:

- **Higher Spiritual Awareness:** As you are still yourself and withdraw your focus from your environment, your attention shifts to whatever you experience in your soul. This higher level of spiritual awareness allows you to find answers to even the most troubling questions. You realize that you have the gift to heal your soul and proceed to do just that during your sessions.

- **Increased Pain Tolerance:** In the beginning, relaxing your mind and body will make you aware of all the pain and discomfort you may feel. However, as you learn to put these aside, your nervous system will start to send fewer pain stimuli to your brain with each session. And since physical pain may be both the cause and the symptoms of a wounded soul, reducing it will put you in higher spirits.
- **Reduced Stress Levels:** When you relax your body and mind, your brain will lower your blood cortisol levels. This hormone causes prolonged effects of stress, including anxiety, depression, lack of sleep, deteriorated cognitive functions, and a whole range of negative emotions that affect your spirit. Eliminating it from the bloodstream means better physical, mental, and spiritual health. At the same time, the levels of the inhibitory neurotransmitter GABA (gamma-aminobutyric acid) in your nervous system increase. This causes all the stress-inducing neurotransmitters to stop functioning, which has the same effect as reducing cortisol levels.
- **Improved Mood:** After each of your sessions, the levels of another hormone, serotonin, will also start increasing. Serotonin is often referred to as the feel-good hormone because it causes a general sense of well-being. Its effects are long-lasting and range across multiple plains of your life. This hormone encourages you to explore negative emotions by making you feel better. No matter how difficult facing them may be, you will be able to do it because you are filled with positive, encouraging emotions.
- **Instant Happiness Booster:** Mediation also promotes the production of endorphins - which, similarly to serotonin, causes a significant mood improvement. And while their euphoric effects don't last as long as the serotonin's, endorphins can give an instant boost when you need it. By receiving a large endorphin dose when communicating with your inner child, you can send them more positive emotions and heal them much sooner.
- **Higher Melatonin Levels:** Focusing your mind during the session will teach you how to eliminate distractions that hinder your body's ability to produce the hormone melatonin. You can triple your melatonin levels in just a few weeks by meditating for only a couple of minutes daily. As a result, you will have much better sleep, a robust immune system, and the ability to prevent many

illnesses known to cause deep-seated spiritual trauma.
- **Elimination of Other Endocrine Causes:** Meditation balances out the levels of insulin and glucagon -the two hormones responsible for regulating blood sugar levels. By maintaining your glucose levels in a normal range, your body receives less stress, which means fewer causes for your spirits to be lower. Meditative practices can also increase your growth hormone levels. This endocrine chemical is responsible for maintaining the proper functions of virtually all the cells in your body. More of it means your ability to prevent physical and mental causes of spiritual imbalance increases.
- **Improved Ability to Express Emotions:** Whether you are experiencing positive or negative feelings, you will be able to convey them in a healthy way just after a few sessions. When you start expressing your emotions, you will notice the positive effects of this act on your relationships. This leads to the production of mood-enhancing hormones discussed previously, enhancing their positive influence on your spiritual wellbeing.
- **Higher Level of Self-Acceptance:** By focusing on giving as much love to your inner child as possible, you are essentially learning how to love and accept yourself. Mediation is an incredible source of nourishment for your soul, an unrivaled confidence booster, and the spiritual benefits of having high confidence levels.
- **Healthier Priorities:** A higher state of awareness can help you rearrange your priorities by placing the healing of your soul at the top of your list. Meditation stimulates your prefrontal cortex- the part of your brain responsible for logical reasoning and thoughts about yourself. The practices can also improve your brain's ability to resist following others in actions, thoughts, and emotions that aren't in alignment with what your inner child feels or wants.

Inner Child Meditation

The following meditation technique is designed to help you reconnect with your inner child and heal them and yourself. It will allow you to see if the child within you is still holding on to painful memories even if they don't want to. It will also help you understand that behind this pain is a child that can show you what happiness truly is. With this exercise, you will learn how to unconditionally love your inner self, honor your deepest wishes, and invite peace into your life.

Here are the steps to do this exercise:

- Start by getting into a comfortable position. You can stand, sit, or even lie down - as long as you can relax your body and mind.
- Close your eyes, take a deep breath, exhale slowly, and repeat.
- Focus on your breathing as you continue to relax until you feel that the rhythm comes naturally.
- When you finally feel that you don't have to concentrate on your breathing anymore, take a mental pause and switch your focus to see if your body is relaxed.
- Check if your cheeks, jaw, and shoulders are relaxed and whether your arms and legs are in a natural position. All your body should feel warm and heavy, except for your stomach area, which should feel light.
- Take another pause and start visualizing your inner child. Take your time to take in their appearance, position, expressions, and demeanor.
- Now open your other senses and try hearing any sounds made by the child, taking in the scents around them, or acknowledging any other stimuli you receive.
- Imagine that the child is holding a dark bubble in one of their hands. Look closer at the dark sphere to see the memories within it.
- Do you sense fear, pain, or sadness in dark memories that appear as still or moving images? Or just floating emotions caused by rejection and disappointment?
- Try to persuade the child to tell you where those emotions come from. More likely than not, your inner child has created elaborate stories about those emotions. If you listen closely, you will notice that these stories resonate with your thoughts.
- In their tale, the child may tell you that they don't feel worthy or good enough to matter to anyone or have what they want. They may also tell you that they've been hurt and can no longer trust others.
- While all of these stories are entirely normal, if you feel that they interfere with your life, now is the time to change them. You can start doing this by taking a deep breath and feeling how the air travels through your body to cleanse it.

- Release the emotions by exhaling deeply and, once again, reach out to the child. Embrace them with positive thoughts and feelings and hold them until you see the dark sphere dissipating in their hands.
- Even if it doesn't disappear completely, tell the child that you accept them even if they can't let go of all the hurt they're in right now. Tell them that they can come to you with any trouble thoughts or emotions they may have in the future.
- Now, take another pause, during which you should only focus on your breathing.
- After that, envision the child again, now with a bright sphere in their other hand. This bubble is filled with happy memories, love, laughter, dreams, and wishes.
- Feel the lightness of these emotions, whether they appear as a picture, a little film, or a simple feeling. Take your time to soak them in and let them fill you with happiness.
- See how happy the child is when they look at the sphere. See how bright their smile is, and let this smile take over you as well.
- Invite more happiness into your life by asking the child about their favorite game, event, or memory.
- Embrace the child again so you can start creating more happy memories and feel their love toward you. It's just as powerful as the one you show toward them.
- When you feel that you and your inner child are now in sync, let their image disappear, bring your attention back to your breathing and return your awareness to the world around you.

Tips for Inner Child Meditation

If you aren't familiar with meditation and other mindfulness techniques, you may find the experience somewhat peculiar. One of the aspects you may struggle with at the beginning of your journey is focusing your mind long enough for the exercise to start working. Fortunately, whatever your inner child wants to say to you, they will get to it as soon as you establish the connection. So, if you haven't been able to understand their message in the first few minutes, sitting for an hour and trying to decipher what your inner child said won't help. It's better to reach out to them another time. If you are dealing with a pressing matter, you can try to reach out to your inner child later on the same day, and if your inquiry can wait, do it the day after your first attempt. The human brain simply can't focus on the same topic for hours because the effects of the beneficial hormones produced during meditation don't last that long. You can start as little as 2-3 minutes at a time and slowly increase the duration of the exercise as your ability to focus improves. With practice, you'll be able to establish an open line of communication with your inner child - and with their help, you will be able to heal yourself from the inside out.

If you want to improve your ability to communicate with your inner child, you should start by choosing the right time of the day for it. Due to the nature of the human circadian rhythm and the brain's tendency to process stimuli and events during sleep, the best time for meditation is early morning. Provided you have a restful night of sleep, meditating right after waking up means you are working with a relaxed, well-rested mind. This will allow you to focus your thoughts without the distractions of the day. Avoid having breakfast before meditation, as digestion itself can be a distraction.

Morning benefits notwithstanding, you can consult your inner child any time during the day. For example, you may find yourself unable to sleep due to troubling ideas about an event. In this case, even focusing on hidden thoughts about the subject for a few minutes at bedtime can give you the clarity you need to have a restful night.

Chapter 6: Inner Child Journaling

This chapter discusses journaling, another technique geared towards uncovering patterns in your current life that have origins in your past. You can step back in time and explore your inner child's pain through journaling. This practice can be valuable when dealing with deep-rooted traumas you can't or won't acknowledge through other methods. That said, before you start recording your emotions, thoughts, and memories in a journal, you should understand what journaling entails and the challenges and benefits of it. Besides empowering you with knowledge about inner child journaling, this chapter will also provide you with a simple journaling guide and a few pieces of advice on how to get the most out of it.

Journaling is an effective technique for healing.
https://pixabay.com/es/photos/computadora-port%c3%a1til-libro-cuero-420011/

What Is Wounded Soul Journaling?

Journaling is the process of exploring your thoughts and emotions and working your way to their effects by writing them down. Having your beliefs recorded on paper makes it easier to recall them. Once written, all you need to do is read them to analyze or remember their significance anytime you feel the need to do so. On paper, even the most confusing experiences get a clearer outlook. The ability to discover the proper perspective makes journaling a very effective coping strategy and a powerful tool for healing your inner child. Journaling through your inner child is designed to help you see every event in the way the child within you experiences them. This will enable you to understand how these experiences impact your spiritual health.

There are many forms of inner child journaling, but the most effective ones are geared toward uncovering specific memories. These typically involve visualizing yourself as a child at the age when these memories were formed. If you aren't sure when the painful memories were created, you should ask your inner child about them first. And when you have the answer to this question, you can move on to the exploration phase.

The Impact of Journaling on Healing Your Inner Child

If you aren't used to expressing your thoughts verbally or on paper, you may find journaling a trying experience. Many people think of journaling as they do about most school or work assignments - another task that must be completed during the day. You may be wondering what good it does to recite your negative thoughts and feelings in your head and put them on paper.

Another challenge you face in this modern world is finding writing on paper an old-fashioned way to communicate, even if it's with your inner self. With all the digital technology around us, we have come to rely on video, voice, and other means of communication. One of the greatest appeals of journaling lies in its ability to remove all the distractions of the digital age - and dissipate the stress that comes with them.

Writing down the possible sources of your issues is only part of the inner child's journaling journey. The other part is learning how to be grateful for every spiritual gift you receive in life. As you write about what your inner child is revealing to you in your visions, you'll slowly discover that everything happens for a reason. Even your negative experiences were nothing more than lessons you can learn from. And as you contemplate the meaning of these crucial lessons, everything you've experienced will be placed in a different perspective. The pain that followed the negative experiences goes away and is replaced by hope, joy, and gratitude - much to your inner child's happiness. You are the creator of your own well-being; journaling will help you understand this. Here are some of the most precious gifts you receive when you journal for your inner child:

- **Reduced Stress Levels:** Writing about what's bothering you in your day-to-day life leads to a long-term decrease in the production levels of the stress inducing-hormone cortisol. It also stimulates the release of neurotransmitters with a similar effect and disrupts pain signals. This will result in lowered blood pressure and improved liver functions, lessening the impact of stress on your physical and mental health.
- **Managing Stress in a Healthy Way:** Even if you initially can't identify the sources or triggers for your anxiety - through journaling - you can learn how to manage your condition in a healthy way. Simply expressing your thoughts about stressful or traumatic experiences will help you avoid resorting to unhealthy distractions and addictive behavior.
- **Improved Immune Response:** When your body doesn't have to combat the effects of stress, it can focus on providing sufficient protection from pathogens. Regular journaling boosts the production of T-lymphocytes, the cells responsible for the processes involved in a healthy immune response. Your wounds will heal faster; you will rebound from colds more quickly, become more productive and acquire a better outlook on life.
- **Learning How to Appreciate Different Experiences:** By discovering what makes you happy, you will learn how to appreciate the simple things in life - as they are often the most important ones. When coming in the right direction, even the smallest gesture or sign can lead to an enormous boost in serotonin production.
- **Improved Mood:** The ability to express your thoughts, even if you can only do it on paper, will boost the production of serotonin and endorphins, chemicals responsible for making you feel good about yourself and your abilities. It also promotes the production of the neurotransmitters responsible for counteracting

signals that spread negative responses throughout your body and mind.
- **Sharper Cognitive Skills:** It's a well-known fact that regular writing and reading promote the honing of cognitive skills, such as your ability to memorize things and recall them later on. By producing inhibitory neurotransmitters and feel-good hormones, your body creates more space for everything needed to keep your cognitive functions in top shape.
- **Increased Confidence Levels:** When the limitations of anxiety and stress no longer bind you, your confidence levels will soar, further contributing to the production of the beneficial hormones that keep your physical, mental, and spiritual health in check.
- **Enhanced Emotional Functions:** Expressing your emotions helps you process them, regardless of their origins or impact on your life. Journaling allows you to connect with your inner needs - enabling you to see which emotions you have used, and which should be discarded after the initial processing phase. Compartmentalizing negative feelings leaves enough room for developing positive ones that carry long-term benefits for your health and happiness.
- **Promotes Self-Discovery:** Through writing, you'll discover what makes you sad and what causes you joy, encouraging you to seek different experiences and learn more about yourself. You will notice the subtle changes caused by each positive event or emotion. This will also help you figure out your purpose and next step toward reaching it.
- **Improved Social Connections**: By developing a more realistic map of your feelings, you will learn how to manage the emotions you express towards others. It will also teach you how to deal with the emotional responses you receive from your environment, encouraging you to develop stronger interpersonal relationships.

Inner Child Journaling

While keeping a journal can seem like a lot of work, it doesn't necessarily have to be. By following this simple guide, you can get to know your inner child and reveal the pain they are hiding in no time.

Here is what you should do:
1. Start by finding a space where you won't be disturbed for at least 20 minutes.
2. Prepare your journal and a pen and place them beside you as you sit comfortably.
3. Relax your shoulders, close your eyes, and visualize your inner child. Try to make the image as vivid as possible, as this will help you with the next step.
4. State your intention in your mind or out loud. Here you can ask your inner child about the emotions or thoughts you can't understand, or you can request guidance for spiritual development.
5. Release your intention by exhaling deeply and waiting for a response.
6. Keep an open mind about what you might receive - the answers may not arrive in the way you may expect them to.
7. Listen to your inner child's message, and don't forget to express your gratitude for their assistance.
8. Open your eyes and write down what you've learned immediately after receiving it. This will help you memorize the advice or instructions. By doing so, you will be able to honor it as closely as possible in the future.
9. After recording the message, take a deep breath and bring your focus back to the present.

Of course, following these steps will only be helpful if you have a clear intention and know which questions you should ask your inner child. Here are some great examples of how to comply with both of these requirements:

- Think about the activities you enjoyed as a child and whether you stopped doing them. If yes, ask your inner child why you shy away from that particular activity.
- Describe a situation in which you felt uncomfortable as a child and consider what you would tell your former self about this.
- Make sure to ask about the most trying thing you went through as a child and how you can release the pain caused by this event.
- Think about a place that made you feel safe as a child, and ask yourself whether you still feel the same way about them.

- Ask your inner child about favorite books, music, movies they like, and the heroes they admire.
- Inquire about your inner child's relationship with childhood friends and family members to see if any of them hurt you, causing you to internalize your feelings.
- Ask if someone else hurt you and whether you forgive them.
- Consider your current outlook on life and compare it to your childhood memories. Pay attention to differences in dreams and aspirations and what caused the changes.
- Ask your inner child if they are afraid of or anxious about something and what you can do to alleviate their fears.
- Ask the child how to treat them and provide them with the love they need to heal both of you.

Additional Tips for Inner Child Journaling

You can journal any time of the day you feel the need to, but for the best result, it's recommended to do this either after waking up or right before going to bed. Your mind will typically be confronted with numerous unanswered questions before going to sleep. Exploring and recording your insecurities, fears, or memories of old trauma before bedtime will help you put all those unanswered questions to rest. This will allow you to sleep better during the night and be healthier and more productive during the day. If any of the questions remain unanswered, your mind may resolve them on its own by processing the information you've got from your inner child.

You can also journal in the morning if you still have troubling thoughts or emotions when you wake up. If you are skeptical about the benefits of inner child journaling, performing the practice at least twice a day should help you notice its benefits soon enough. In fact, you don't even have to wait until bedtime or morning to journal. You can do it anytime you feel that you have to eliminate something from your system, even if you aren't sure what this is. You don't have to carry your journal with you all the time, either. Just keep a pen and a piece of paper with you so you can perform a quick inquiry and write down whatever you received as a response. You can copy this later in your journal so it can allow you to reread it carefully and contemplate its meaning.

You don't have to be a professional writer or possess creative writing skills to start journaling. Your entries don't have to be anything formal, just relevant to the questions you are asking your inner child. This means that you only need to write whatever association your brain makes first. Avoid contemplating the meaning of what you experience during the visualization process. Instead, document anything that comes to mind first, as honestly and succinctly as possible. If you find it easier to record the message or parts of it in pictures, feel free to draw it, starting from your inner child. Pay attention to the child's appearance, demeanor, and physical environment.

Creating a vivid image of your inner child helps focus your intention on them and will make it easier to draw your inner child in your journal next to some crucial entries. By immortalizing the child in your journal, you are creating tangible evidence of your eternal connection. Looking at their image will allow you to form a deeper bond, decipher their messages and prepare for other ones in the future. Draw the inner child in color to prevent your clear view of them from fading. Make sure to add any detail that stands out, such as an object they are holding or even a reference to the place or item they are showing you in their message. This is recommended for beginners who struggle with deciphering the meaning of spiritual messages if they have them written down in a journal. You don't necessarily have to draw a picture when communicating with your inner child. However, doing it as often as you can helps you understand their struggles so you can make them (and yourself) happier.

Journaling can be combined with other techniques, such as meditation, mindfulness, spiritual awareness, and affirmation techniques. Incorporating positive affirmations into your journaling practice will encourage you to give your inner child all the love they deserve. Right after you express your gratitude for the answer or guidance you received, you can say something like this:

> "Now, I release the negativity from my body, mind, and soul.
>
> I'm happy to let go of all these things and move on.
>
> The wounds on my soul will only encourage me to become the best version of myself.
>
> I believe myself capable of everything I put my mind to - including letting go of unhealthy situations and undeserving people.
>
> I free myself from all these things because I deserve to be happy."

Initially, one journal should suffice for all your thoughts. However, after practicing it for a while, you may want to think about two separate journals. In one, you can record all your negative emotions and troubling thoughts. The second one should be the place for expressing gratitude for all the positivity you experience. In the beginning, you should simply start your entries with the negative aspects and end them with the positive ones in the same journal. Try imagining your life as a journey with obstacles and rewards - all of which you encounter for a specific reason. Whether some hurt you or made you feel better, accept it and move on. Whatever material and spiritual gifts you receive, be grateful for them. Remember that not everyone is so lucky to have all those things. After all, healing your wounded inner child is accepting yourself for who you are, what you have, and what you can do with your newfound spiritual gifts.

After a while, your relationship with your inner child will improve - and you will learn to decipher their messages immediately. You won't need to read your entries about your experiences a couple of times to understand them, as you probably have to do when you start journaling. Not only that, but with enough practice, after writing down all the negative things, you will be able to move to the second part - expressing your gratitude for everything you have experienced (good or bad) when visualizing your inner child.

Chapter 7: Inner Child Awareness

Do you think you are self-aware? Most people will answer "yes" because they aren't really familiar with the concept of self-awareness. However, experiencing true self-awareness is rare; only a few people know who they are and are rarely attuned to different parts of their personalities. Your wounded soul is a part of your true self, so when you become self-aware, you achieve inner child awareness as well.

Awareness is being present in the here and now without any concerns about the past or worries about the future. Most of us are never really "present" or living in the moment; our minds are always wandering somewhere else. This is the result of living a fast-paced life and always thinking of what we are going to do next. When was the last time you were truly focused on what you were doing? Do you remember the last time you drank coffee and were fully aware of the taste and the smell? When you go for a walk, are you aware of your legs moving and your heart beating? Or are you thinking only of the destination?

Your inner child lives in your unconscious mind, where all your past trauma and experiences are stored. We rarely pay attention to it, although it can help us learn so much about ourselves. Through awareness, you will be able to recognize negative emotions like anxiety or anger and access the subconscious mind to find their origins. This will help you manage these emotions instead of suppressing them or letting them take over. If you aren't aware and focused on your inner self and the world around you, you will not be able to pay attention to your inner child and heal its pain.

Inner child awareness is being able to focus inward on your emotions, thoughts, and actions and how they relate to your wounded soul. It usually raises the question, "Do my actions and thoughts align with what I am truly feeling?" This can lead you to determine if what you are feeling is the result of your inner child taking over or not. Some people are naturally self-aware and attuned to their inner self and inner child. They can easily evaluate their emotions and understand their triggers which can help them manage their reactions and be in control.

Being aware of your inner child will help you objectively perceive your emotions. Simply put, you will not be mad at your inner child or feel guilty or ashamed of it. You will be objective and understanding of your wounded soul's pain. Even after you discover your inner child, you may not be truly aware of it at all times. You may not always interpret it as your inner child behind certain actions, especially in the heat of the moment. However, when you practice inner child awareness, you can check on yourself to see where these feelings are coming from.

Inner child awareness will play a huge role in your healing as it will enable you to constantly check on your wounded soul during the day to see if it is happy, sad, or triggered by something. You will also be aware of your wounded child's strengths and weaknesses and how your actions impact the people in your life as well. This awareness will motivate you to take advantage of your strengths to grow and work on your weaknesses to heal.

Naturally, you will be curious about its reactions and triggers after connecting with your inner child. For instance, if you always tense up or feel anxious around a sibling or a family member, you may find these feelings confusing, and you will want to explore them to get to their roots. Inner child awareness will help you tap into your memories and realize that this family member may be used to bully or belittle you as a child, which is why you feel nervous every time you are around them. That said, being aware of your inner child can also help you experience more positive childhood feelings like joy or feeling carefree.

When we become aware of our inner child, we may experience feelings of guilt because we have neglected this wounded part of ourselves for so long. However, we will also sympathize with it and begin treating it with more love and compassion.

To always be aware and focused, you should practice awareness in every aspect of your life, like walking, sitting, eating, breathing, etc. Once you become aware of the world around you and the world within you, it will be easier for you to pay attention and stay focused on your inner child.

We have mentioned in previous chapters that our inner child wants attention and is always trying to communicate with us its needs. Are you listening to your inner child? Do you understand it is asking for help? Inner child awareness will open your senses so you can listen to your wounded soul when it is in pain and needs tending to. You can embrace it and let it know you will no longer neglect it. You can do this through writing, speaking to it, or even crying if this is going to be therapeutic.

The Positive Impact of Inner Child Awareness

According to research psychologist and author Diana Raab, inner child awareness will help you remember simpler times and the joy and innocence of childhood. When you tap into these emotions, you will be able to handle many of the challenges you face as an adult.

Discovering your inner child isn't easy for some people. Realizing a part of yourself is wounded can be hard, so instead of working on themselves to heal, they choose to suppress their feelings and ignore their inner child altogether. However, with awareness, you will be able to recognize this part of yourself rather than fight it. We can use awareness to embrace our inner child as well to give it the validation it has always wanted. Additionally, awareness requires you to be focused and present, enabling you to recognize the source of your pain and take the appropriate steps toward your healing.

Simply put, inner child awareness helps you recognize your inner child, embrace it, and heal it. Focusing on your daily activities will make looking inward and having better insight into your inner child easier.

Practicing awareness has always played a huge role in helping people heal from their trauma. You may be angry, sad, or hurt, but you aren't aware of it because you don't pay attention to your feelings or thoughts. As you become more conscious and aware of your inner self, you will be better equipped to work on your healing. In fact, various scientific studies have shown the benefits of awareness on our mental health and improving our wellbeing.

Our wounded inner child may be suffering from various mental health issues like depression, anxiety, stress, or trauma. Practicing awareness can improve your mental health so your inner child can heal from its past experiences and trauma.

Reduces Anxiety and Stress

Do you suffer from anxiety every time you have to speak in public, attend family gatherings, or stand up for yourself? This can be the result of a traumatic experience in your childhood. When you are aware of being anxious and stressed, you can consciously choose to work on your anxiety or lower your stress levels. You can achieve this by responding differently when you are stressed or working on remaining in control of your emotions rather than letting them control you and act out as a result.

Become Empathetic toward Your Inner Child

Inner child awareness allows you to be attuned to what your wounded soul is always feeling, especially when it is hurting and asking for help. This vulnerable part of yourself wants its feelings to be validated. By becoming aware of its pain, you will show empathy toward this broken part inside of you. Once you become empathetic, you will be more understanding of your inner child's needs to work on meeting these needs and thus healing.

Make Better Decisions

We have discussed in previous chapters how your inner child affects your decisions. As you become more aware of your wounded soul, you will better understand where your decisions are coming from. You will know if a decision stems from your inner child's fear or your adult self. Realizing your trauma is the driving source behind some of your reckless decisions will help you make better ones with a clear mind and without being influenced by your pain.

Self-Control

Your inner child is driven by pain and anger. Just like a child, it has no control over its emotions and throws tantrums every chance it gets. Inner child awareness will help you know when your thoughts, feelings, and reactions are irrational. Therefore, instead of reacting or losing your temper, you will take control of your emotions and respond rationally and calmly instead.

Change Bad Habits

As a result of your trauma, your wounded soul has acquired bad habits like self-criticism, belittling yourself, and the inability to say no. Being aware of your inner child will help you notice these habits, so you can change your thought patterns and, thus, your habits. For instance, if a friend asks you to pick them up from the airport but you have a job interview, your inner child will influence you to say yes because you are a people pleaser. However, by practicing inner child awareness, you will realize that you don't have to say yes to everything, especially when it inconveniences you. You will be aware that your inner child is afraid of standing up to itself and saying no. So, you will set healthy boundaries and learn when to say yes and when to say no without feeling guilty.

Change Your Perspective and Thought Patterns

Your inner child is still stuck in the past with the same childlike personality, looking at the world from the perspective of a scared and vulnerable kid. Because your thoughts haven't evolved or changed since you were a child, you may not be aware there is something wrong with the way you think or see the world. After you discover your inner child and embrace it, you can practice inner child awareness, tap into its thought pattern, and learn more about yourself and your inner child's pain. Whenever you have a negative thought, instead of giving in to it, take control and try to figure out what has brought these thoughts on. Are they the result of unrealistic worries? Do they stem from your pain and trauma? Once you take control and change your thought patterns, you can replace negative thoughts with more rational and positive ones.

Inner Child Awareness Guide

Practicing self-awareness isn't only effective, but it is also very easy and a great tool you can implement in your life to heal your inner child. In the next part of the chapter, we will provide simple exercises you can practice every day in various situations, so you are always aware of your inner child.

Ask Yourself Why

Before you make any decision, ask yourself, "Why am I making this decision?" and write down your answer. Give yourself a moment, ask yourself the same question a second and then a third time, and write down your answers. Take a look at the answers; are they rational? Are they good reasons? Do they stem from fear? Your answers will make it clear if you are making the right decision or influenced by your inner child's fear.

When your decisions are based on facts, you will feel confident with your choices and make better ones in life. The more you practice this technique, the more it will become second nature to you, and you will ask yourself the three whys each time. This will prevent your inner child from taking over whenever you're about to make a big decision.

Saying No to Your Inner Child

Your inner child should be treated with love and compassion, but just like a real child, you can't indulge in its every need. When you are aware of your inner child, you can tell the difference between your adult's self-demands and your wounded soul's demands. When you have unhealthy or irrational thoughts, this can be your inner child asking for something. You should only satisfy its health needs. For instance, if it wants you to turn to food to satisfy your emotional needs, throw a tantrum when your partner cancels a date, or spend money with no concern for the future, you should act like a strict parent and say "no."

Inner child awareness helps you see the difference between a child's needs and a mature person's needs. You will learn to reprogram your brain and re-parent your inner child by saying no to temptations and replacing bad or unhealthy thoughts and needs with healthy ones.

Think Before You Act

You have probably been told to think before you act. For many people, this is easier said than done. However, it can still be done with practice. Just like the three "whys" we have mentioned above to help you think before you make a decision, you should also pause and reflect before you act. Whenever we face a challenging or emotional situation, our inner child takes over and says things we shouldn't.

So, assess the situation and think objectively whenever you feel triggered or frustrated. This can be done by taking a few breaths before reacting to give yourself time to think clearly and assess the situation.

Watch Out for Negative Thoughts

Negative thoughts are the result of our fears and anxieties. They aren't rational, helpful, or have any base in reality. You should always be aware of these thoughts to determine their origin. For instance, if you aren't accepted in a job, you may think you are a failure instead of the more logical thinking that they probably went for someone with more experience. These thoughts stem from your vulnerable inner child, and all the time, a parent or teacher made you feel like you weren't good enough. Even when you achieve something, you will pass it off as luck instead of celebrating your successes.

Pay attention to your thoughts, and work on changing your thought patterns. Every time you achieve something, celebrate it even if you don't feel like it; this will reprogram your brain until celebrating your successes comes naturally to you. You should also forgive yourself and practice self-compassion each time you make a mistake instead of criticizing or being hard on yourself. Being aware of your wounded inner child and its thoughts is the only way to notice its negativity so you can replace them with a positive attitude.

Identify Your Triggers

There is always a reason for feeling anxious, angry, or frustrated during certain situations. In most cases, something has triggered your inner child, which manifested in these feelings. For instance, you feel anxious before every work meeting but don't pay attention to why you feel this way, so you never question it. By practicing inner child awareness, you can become aware of what triggered these feelings of anxiety. Maybe just the thought of having to speak up in a meeting was triggering. It reminded you of all the times you spoke up during family gatherings, and they would either make jokes or dismiss your opinions. By identifying your triggers, your adult self can take over by thinking logically and not letting your inner child use fear to hold you back.

Your triggers can also be a person or a place. Be conscious of your negative emotions and how you respond to your environment. Every time you experience a negative feeling, ask yourself: Why did I feel (angry, jealous, frustrated, sad, etc.) when talking to this person? Did they say something to make me feel this way? How did I react? Have I felt these emotions before? The answers will help you identify if your trigger was the person, tone of voice, or something they said. You can compare this situation to something you experienced in your childhood to understand why you feel this way now. If it is a person or a place that triggers you, you can avoid them, if possible.

Meditation

Meditation is known to help you clear your mind, stay focused, and be present in the here and now. You will find many mediation techniques that require you to be focused on your breathing. Even if you don't have time for meditating, you can simply take a couple of minutes at any time of the day to focus on your breathing. You can practice meditation by focusing on your breathing when you wake up before you go to sleep or in the car before you drive to work. When you focus on your breathing, you will begin to be more mindful and aware of your surroundings and everything you do. We have provided meditation techniques in this book, and you can also find various methods online or download meditation apps.

Evaluate Yourself

Check on yourself every once in a while to see if your inner child awareness is improving or not. You can also write down all the times that awareness has helped your inner child with its healing. Are you more aware, or are you still struggling? You can speak with a therapist if you have difficulty with inner child awareness.

Inner child awareness is an easy and effective method to heal your wounded soul. As you become focused on the present moment, your environment, and your inner child, you will be able to assess your wounded soul's emotions and reactions. Simply put, your inner child will always be on your mind, so you can easily tap into its feelings instead of letting it take over. You will be the one in control.

Chapter 8: The Challenges of Healing Your Inner Child

Did you ever take the time to listen to the random, little voices inside your head? You know, these voices that sound much like the younger version of you? This is what inner child healing is all about. As you know, it doesn't matter how old you get or where life takes you. Your inner child will always be there to accompany you on your life journey. Your inner child, however, will show up whenever you're the most hurt or disappointed. It will resurface when your friend doesn't take your call. Your teenage self may speak louder if you and your friend get into an argument. Taking note of when your inner child makes itself heard and acknowledging what it says are among the most important steps of inner child work.

Inner child work, or healing, is among the most popular methods of addressing the feelings of rejection and the things you believe you lacked throughout your childhood. It is a way to come to terms with the needs your inner child never fulfilled and overcome the attachment wounds you grew up with. Regardless of what your childhood was like, the chances are that there's a younger part of yourself that feels as if no one loved it enough or the right way.

Inner child healing is similar to any type of inner healing. For one, it requires you to give your subconscious the space to guide the process. You need to dig deep into your being and explore your emotions. Inner work urges you to nudge the parts of you that others have forced you to conceal. Growing up, you may have felt the need to suppress certain sides of yourself because of other people's snarky remarks. By permitting yourself to explore yourself from within, you start to tear down your daily coping mechanisms, such as avoidance, isolation, or numbing your emotions. Only then can you accept, acknowledge, and incorporate your subconscious workings into your consciousness.

Inner child healing is commonly used in several types of therapy, including trauma therapy, sensorimotor psychotherapy, narrative therapy, and art therapy. The best thing about this healing approach is that it encourages you to speak to your inner child in the language that it speaks. This means you will need to embody your emotions and let them guide you through these reflective conversations instead of expressing yourself through words and thoughts.

All of us traverse the world with the wounds we've developed throughout childhood. Even the simplest of traumas can affect us in significant ways. Everything, from neglect or emotional rejection to physical abuse, leaves its mark. We were always told to get over it or were made to believe that what we've experienced is "normal." This is why most of us never speak about our past experiences. We are left alone to experience the pain and emotions because "this is what adults are supposed to do."

Inner child work is vital because it always reminds us that our feelings are valid. We need the reassurance that our memory and feelings aren't wrong. It allows us to let the shame go and openly acknowledge these emotions. By healing your inner child, you are healing that little kid who felt neglected and the teen who cried every night because nobody understood them. When you're healing your inner child, you cultivate the safety, protection, and security that your younger child has always yearned for. In doing that, you alleviate some negativity your younger self has experienced, making room for positive experiences to emerge. Your natural, innate gifts, child-driven curiosity, and endless compassion are embraced.

However, avoiding acknowledging your past traumas leaves you feeling stuck and isolated. Repressing them only makes them worse because they will find other harmful ways to come out. Mental health issues and destructive mechanisms, such as alcoholism, substance abuse, workaholism, or even bullying and racism, occur. Inner child problems are often generational. This is why you're not only healing yourself by doing this type of work. You are helping generations learn to make peace with who they essentially are.

In this chapter, we will explore the challenges that come with the process of healing the inner child. You'll learn what to expect and read through some tips on how to work through them. Then, you'll find a multiple-step guide to navigating the challenges of inner child work.

The Challenges of Inner Child Work

Healing your inner child is not an easy endeavor. The process is very long and challenging. Though, many people don't realize that the main issue lies within the fact that the people who have hurt you will never help you heal. As an adult, you probably realize that you must go about this process independently. Healing starts from within, and you're the only one who can help yourself overcome these hardships. However, your subconscious or inner child doesn't grasp that. As a kid, you had complete blind trust in those around you, especially your family and the ones you loved the most. You looked up to them and sought them out for guidance. This is why the kid in you waits for the solution to come *from them*. After all, your parents probably jumped in to help you fix every problem you get yourself into.

You need to help the child in you realize that you need to work with them to heal their wounds. Your subconscious needs to make peace with the fact that there will be no one to come in to apologize and help you pick up the pieces they broke. Most adults will never admit that they hurt you in your childhood. Your parents will likely never acknowledge that they may have wronged you or were unsuccessful in their attempt at parenthood. Fortunately, there are many ways to go on about the heavy responsibility of healing the child within you. But first, let's look at some challenges you may face throughout this journey.

1. **The Lack of Common Trust**

Your inner child has been let down one too many times. They had unquestionable trust in the same people who initially betrayed them. This is why your inner child will not warm up to you easily. Yes, even when you are the older version. We are usually our strongest and most potent enemy. We constantly criticize, shame, and hurt ourselves. You have probably invalidated your emotions or shamed yourself for feeling the way you do at one point in your life. The only way you can get your child to come out of its hiding place is by proving to them that you're their ally and friend. You need to be supportive and non-critical. Most importantly, you need to acknowledge and validate their feelings and everything that they went through, no matter how much society normalizes it. Recognizing your younger self's neglect, abuse, abandonment, and loneliness is essential to healing.

In other words, be the adult that your younger self needs. You were supposed to be cared for while growing up. Instead, you ended up wounded. It's easy to feel like the damage can't be undone, especially when you have no idea where to start. The journey is long, and you need to tackle many aspects of your current and past self. On the other hand, you are an adult now. You need to trust your ability to care for yourself and offer your inner child the type of care that they deserve. Think about what went wrong and the things that hurt you as a child, and what could've made things better for you. For instance, if your parents used to abuse you verbally, your inner child would need someone to respect, encourage, and support them. This is how you need to approach your younger self. Retreat to a quiet place and have a conversation with your inner child out loud. Tell them everything they want to hear. Express your love for your inner child and tell them that you're proud of them.

2. The Need for Validation

It is sometimes hard to separate your own thoughts and feelings from those around you. We are automatically influenced by the mindsets and beliefs of our community. We adopt many ideas as our own even when we don't entirely agree with them. This is why you may still be inclined toward trivializing or even justifying how you were hurt. You will manage to find a reason for the way you were shamed, abandoned, or forced to grow up before your time. You may even tell yourself that your experiences weren't that bad. This is why you need to take a step back and ask yourself whether these claims are coming from your authentic self or are influenced by the world around you. Because if they were your own, you wouldn't be reading this book and trying to figure out how to heal your inner child. If these hurtful actions were justifiable, or what you experienced wasn't "that bad," then you wouldn't feel hurt in the first place. Acknowledge that whatever you've gone through wounded you. If it makes you feel any better, your parents did not nurture you how they had to, not because they're bad people, but because they, too, have wounded inner children.

Make your inner child feel seen and listen to their hardships. Knowing that you're loved and feeling the love are never the same. Your younger self needs to feel the love. It needs to know that people see who they really are and understand that they are cared for. It's up to you to do so. Fortunately, there is plenty you can do to make up for that now that you're no longer a child. Think about how your inner child reacts in the face of challenges, fears, the things that make them happy, etc. Be attentive to them.

3. Dealing with the Stages of Grief

Shock and anger are the beginning stages of grief, which, believe it or not, is a sign that you're heading in the right direction. Anger and shock are very normal feelings, even if you understand that whatever you've experienced in your childhood was never intentional. Anger is a standard element in the inner wounded child healing process. You don't need to break things or scream at the top of your lungs (however, if you need to, that's fine too), but it's your right to be very mad.

If you think about it, your parents probably did the best job any two adults with a wounded inner child can do. However, this doesn't mean that you're any less emotionally and spiritually hurt by how things went down. This is exactly why you need to realize that it's up to you to hold a generation of wounded children accountable to stop hurting themselves and those around them.

Stand up for the younger version of you whenever someone offends or belittles them in any way. Now, it wouldn't be possible to travel back in time (although that would accelerate the healing process or even deflect the damage), but you can stand up for yourself right now, especially when someone belittles you in a way that your inner child was used to. For instance, if you were frequently told how dramatic you were, then be sure to stand up for yourself if someone says that to you now. Let them know their limits and explain that this is something you don't appreciate hearing. Make your inner child proud to know that you no longer tolerate any type of disrespect.

4. The Waves of Sadness

You will inevitably experience deep waves of anger and sadness after you're done feeling angry. You'll likely grieve the life you could've lived if you weren't still dealing with the consequences of your past wounds. You'll feel a sense of regret regarding all your childhood dreams, ambitions, and aspirations. It's okay to grieve the unfulfillment of everything that you haven't developed healthily.

It helps involve your inner child in your journey. After all, you need their cooperation to make it past the healing phase. By now, you should be able to tell what makes your inner child happy. You don't need to have everything covered, nor do you need to know everything about your inner child. This entire journey is a learning experience. This means you'll find something new about your younger self every day. Use your scope of knowledge to do the things your inner child likes as frequently as you can. It's easy to ignore your inner child when trying to become the adult you "ought to be." What we don't realize, however, is that this worsens the situation. The more we repress the desires of our inner child, the more prominent they become. Eventually, you won't be able to push them aside, as they will leave you feeling irritated, relentless, and hopeless. If you've been doing that for a long time, you may even end up experiencing an identity crisis. This is a sign that you need to align your behavior with your needs.

5. Remorse Kicks In

Remorse is a very strong emotion that kicks in whenever we've lost something. It is often experienced after the loss of a loved one. However, it is also relevant in your case because your inner child may start to wonder if they could've done anything differently. You need to help your subconscious realize the fact that there was nothing that your younger self could've done to change how things went down. Let your inner child know that their pain should be about them and not what could've been. They were never responsible for what they went through. They couldn't have been a better child to their parents. It was their job to give your inner child a healthy upbringing, and it's your job, as an adult, to let your inner child know just that.

6. You'll Feel Lonely

Perhaps the strongest feelings you'll experience throughout this journey are profound shame and loneliness. Your parents abandoning or abusing you is shameful to you. You feel bad about yourself and likely believe that there's something wrong with you because this is how they treated you. This shame eventually leads to loneliness. Your inner child feels like they're an alien. They feel contaminated, and so they will hide their authentic self from the world, putting on a mask in the process. Your inner child lives the rest of his life as an imposter, which makes them feel lonely and misunderstood.

This is the last and longest step in the healing process. It is the most challenging to endure. However, there is a way out, which is to seek therapy. You need to reach out to a professional to deal with your shame and loneliness healthily. These feelings are hard to acknowledge on our own. Though, acknowledgment and acceptance are necessary if you want to overcome these obstacles. It is the only way you'll finally reconnect with your long-lost true self.

Navigate the Challenges of Inner Child Healing

The following is a multiple-step guide you can use to navigate the challenges that come with inner child work:

1. **Acknowledge Your Inner Child**

If you want to start healing, you must acknowledge that your inner child is there and hurting. Be open to the idea of exploring the past, so you don't further complicate the healing process. You may struggle with approaching your younger self at first. This is why it helps to explore your most significant childhood experiences first. Accept that they happened, dig deep into how they made you feel, and then talk to your inner child as if they were a real, separate person.

2. **Be an Active Listener**

Listen to the feelings that arise during your conversation. Be attentive to emotions like anger, loneliness, insecurity, shame, anxiety, and guilt, and interpret what they are trying to say to you. Try to trace them back to some events or even people in your life. Think about the situations that trigger similar emotions in your adult self. Do you sense a pattern?

3. **Try Journaling or Writing a Letter**

Now that you're grown, you probably have a different perspective than you did back then, especially when it comes to the events or situations that wounded you. Writing them down can help you address the things your inner child doesn't fully grasp. Let's say you may have always feared your brother because he was an angry child. If you now know that he was subject to years of bullying, you may help your inner child understand that your brother's anger was never against the child in you. Ask your inner child about their feelings and how they would like you to support them.

4. **Meditate**

Now that you've asked your inner child some questions, it is time to meditate. This will help you bring answers to light. Meditation is known to heighten a person's self-awareness by teaching you to direct your focus to the emotions that arise during the day. Meditation is all about mindfulness, which makes it easier to spot the events that trigger unwanted actions.

Loving your inner child doesn't happen overnight, nor does healing your wounds. You may not realize it now; however, once you embark on the healing journey, you will realize that inner child work is all about loving the younger version of yourself. It doesn't matter how odd, shy, difficult, annoying, loud, or weird you thought (or were told) you were. You did, and you still deserve love. You don't need a time machine to return and let your inner child know they are worth the world.

Chapter 9: The Benefits of Healing Your Inner Child

Connecting with your inner child can do wonders. It may sound like an exaggeration; however, you can transform your life by healing that little kid inside you. You will never fully realize how much your wounded inner child was holding you back until you completely heal. You will look back and wonder how you were traversing life with that much weight strapped to your shoulders.

Inner child work allows you to forgive and move forward. You learn to acknowledge what your parents did to you without blaming them for the way you turned out. Healing your inner child comes with a different level of maturity where you don't deny the impact of your upbringing but still understand that this is the best your parents could've done. The healing process will help you come to terms with the fact that there's nothing you could've done to stop this from happening. When all the work is done, you will see that you are responsible for taking the initiative and changing certain aspects of your life. You simply don't have to settle for the way things are. You will no longer be a victim of your own sadness or experiences, nor will you allow yourself to be overtaken by feelings of resentment, which leads us to the next point.

Inner child work is empowering. It will urge you not to allow self-doubt and fear to guide you. Instead, you will learn to take the reins when it comes to your emotions and reactions. A great part of healing your inner child depends on how you defend your current and younger selves whenever you need to. You would no longer use your past traumas as excuses to indulge in destructive behaviors. This type of healing will help you let go of your old, unwanted habits. When you're empowered, you will no longer want to live as a victim who blames their destructive coping mechanisms on their past traumas.

The healing process comes with its fair share of pain and discomfort. However, if there's one thing you'll learn, it's that the greatest amount of healing comes when you're outside of your comfort zone. In this chapter, you'll learn about the benefits of healing your inner child and how you can achieve them. Here, you will also find a quiz that will help you pinpoint which benefits you have experienced by practicing healing your wounded soul.

Benefits of Inner Child Work

No matter what you do, nothing will stop you from acting like a child unless you do some serious inner child work. No amount of anger or time management, breathing, or meditative techniques will help you improve your attention, acknowledge and control your emotions, and hold yourself accountable instead of blaming and accusing others, communicating effectively, and jumping to conclusions. Although these techniques can offer great complimentary support, you must first address your main problem: healing your wounded inner child. Once you start healing your inner child, you'll witness your life-changing right before your eyes. You may feel pressured to do everything by the book. However, in this journey, no one is perfect. There isn't a standard healing practice that you can benchmark your efforts against in the first place. As long as you're connecting with your inner child, validating their emotions, and being the parent they deserve and long for, you will be able to reap the benefits of self-love, compassion, self-awareness, and emotional control. The following are some of the benefits of doing inner child work:

1. **Acknowledging the Pain**

You will never truly understand the pain and the extent of its impact unless you hear from the wounded. You need to create a safe space for them to talk about how they feel as they reflect on their emotions. You can do that by prioritizing safety in the relationship you build with your inner child. Make them feel safe, loved, and important. Approach them with respect and validation so they can warm up to you. Only then can you penetrate the layers of accumulated wounds, reflecting on each revelation you make. Take it slow and work at your inner child's pace. Never push boundaries or go beyond your and your inner child's pain thresholds. Otherwise, you will compromise that trust.

2. Exploring Your Boundaries

There are many aspects to healing your inner child. It's a very dynamic journey. Your feelings, needs, and desires may change multiple times throughout the process, depending on the traumas, memories, and experiences you encounter. You must remember that you're working with your inner child throughout the years. For instance, your emotional and developmental needs at the age of 6 are quite different from your needs at the age of 14. Whenever you're working with your inner child, make sure to take note of their emotional age. Then, generate your boundaries, tailoring them to each version of yourself. Regardless of what your needs are, approach them without judgment.

Exploring your boundaries throughout the years gives you a lot of insight into the person you are today. It helps you better understand your needs, preferences, and dislikes. It will also help you determine what your current boundaries are in life.

3. Working Your Way toward Wholeness

If you're struggling with a wounded inner child, you haven't experienced wholeness yet. Unresolved pains and traumas make it impossible for you to find and embrace all parts of yourself. You lead your life in fragments of your being. Have you ever noticed how it's easy for you to set aside a part of yourself whenever you have to? Healing your inner child is a lot like searching for a lost kid. You look everywhere, trying to trace the steps back and putting clues together until you finally find them. You achieve wholeness when you've successfully brought back the child and found that it coexists harmoniously with your adult self. While it's easier said than done, the only piece of advice we can give you here is to sit tight. Patience is a virtue. You embarked on this journey knowing that it won't be easy. Whenever you feel like you want to give up, remember why you started in the first place. Think of the child who deserved better growing up. Remind yourself that you can't let them down again.

4. Identifying Narcissism

Many of those who experience childhood trauma end up falling victim to narcissistic abuse and toxic relationships. This is often a survivor's coping method or trauma response. This is especially the case if you grew up with narcissistic caregivers who desensitized you to this type of unacceptable behavior. Being constantly exposed to it as a child probably led you to believe that it was normal. A significant aspect of inner child work is understanding your trauma response patterns. You will learn a lot about safe and toxic relationships when you discover how they developed in the first place and how they helped you in life. This will make it easier for you to spot narcissists and avoid falling into the same traps.

5. No More Tantrums

If you are yet to heal your inner child, then the occasional emotional meltdown is probably no stranger to you. Keeping track of your triggers and tracing them back to certain memories, correlations, stories, or events can help you break the emotional outburst cycle before it occurs. Suppose someone, for instance, says something that you now realize would trigger an undesirable reaction. In that case, you should be ready to distract your inner child or deflect their reaction. Going for a long walk, retreating to a safe space, meditating, or doing breathing exercises are all preventative measures. It will take some experimentation until you find something that works for the child inside.

"Paradoxical anger" is another type of anger. Every time you were angry with your parents, you probably repressed your emotions. Your feelings weren't something that you could easily express because lashing out would've come with consequences. Unfortunately, the same people who compromised your boundaries, sense of security, and trust are the ones that your younger self depended on. As you do inner child work, you need to find positive ways in which you can release the repressed anger while preventing emotional outbursts.

As you may recall from the previous chapter, you need to take the time to explore your inner child's wants and desires. Figure out what makes them happy, calm, and relaxed. This would give your insight into the activities you need to do to prevent outbursts.

6. Attaining Freedom from Toxic Shame

Think about your current life and reflect on your life as a teenager. What are the thoughts that preoccupy your brain? When you think about yourself as a child, what comes to mind? Is it a shame? Feelings of inadequacy?

How often do you catch yourself shaming your younger self? You may find yourself reflecting on how imperfect you were and how you could've done better to make your parents proud. Maybe you think of all the rash decisions you took when you were 16 and all the things you did that didn't match your values. The only way to free yourself from toxic shame is to externalize these emotions. Talking about your past can help you get rid of the shame and replace it with compassion.

7. Being Your Own Parent

When you're doing inner child work, you must treat your inner child as a child of your own. You need to nurture it and care for it. This means you can be the parent you lacked as a child. You get to do things right this time around, ensuring that you meet your younger self's developmental needs. Be the person your inner child can depend on, connect with, and confide in. You are their only shot at getting heard, finding safety, and feeling loved unconditionally.

8. Breaking Unhealthy Cycles

Have you ever wondered why it's often those who had unstable childhoods are the ones that end up in codependent and unhealthy relationships? Well, it's because people with somewhat similar struggles are subconsciously attracted to each other. They are drawn to what's familiar, and together, they relive moments from their childhoods.

As children, we were helpless and completely dependent on our parents. We looked up to them and believed that they were always right. This is why we automatically thought it was our fault when troubles arose. We came up with beliefs and assumptions about ourselves that we carried into adulthood. We also created strategies that we thought would help us get whatever we needed from our parents. We still resort to these strategies in all our relationships. We inadvertently recreate the chaos we grew up with to ensure that our behaviors, thoughts, and actions are still relevant. Knowing what to expect and maintaining a sense of familiarity provide us with a false sense of safety and security.

You need to discover which patterns you fall into to make a conscious choice. While it will be extremely uncomfortable at first, you must go out of your comfort zone to show your inner child that you don't need to recreate the same environment they were brought up in or refer to the same strategies to be safe.

9. Determining Your Self-Worth

Unfortunately, we live in a world where our value is determined by what we do rather than who we are. The world is utterly role-based. It's sad to see that families – where members are supposed to have unconditional love and respect for each other – follow the same construct.

From a young age, we are taught to let go of our individuality and set aside our hobbies, talents, and complete identities so we can adopt traits that would make our parents proud. We are encouraged to appeal to the world instead of being ourselves.

Our parents taught us that the things we like and love (the things that essentially make us who we are) come second to our "role." You probably spent your whole childhood trying to perfect the role that they had mapped out for you. You did your best to overachieve, whether it came to your academics, athletics, or chores, thinking that this was what you wanted. Unfortunately, being an overachiever is seldom a personal choice. It rather sprouts from the need to please one's parents. If you have an older sibling, then they're probably the ones who ended up on the overachiever train. Though, this probably didn't salvage you from unnecessary emotional damage. Instead of feeling pressured to excel at every aspect of life, you had to hear about what a "star" your sibling is, which likely made you feel inferior or useless.

Inner child work is your shot at making your inner child feel worthy and valued. You need to address your inner child using positive statements, highlighting how valuable their authentic self is. Explore your inner child's dreams and aspirations, comparing them to your parents' standards. Do you really want to be the person you strived to be? Reassure your inner child that they were born with a much greater purpose that only their unique and special gifts can help them fulfill.

10. Discovering Who You Truly Are

As we just explained, taking on that designated role cuts off your connection with the person you truly are. The moment you made it your mission to do everything you could to please your parents, you wiped out fragments of your being. The playful, curious, creative, imaginative, and spontaneous parts of yourself were diminished. You no longer carried around the healthy sense of shamelessness, innocence, and objectivity that every child should have. At a very young age, you were introduced to the concepts of self-criticism, guilt, and shame.

You need to take the time to reconnect with the younger version of yourself. Take as long as it takes to remember who you once were. Remember the kid who was not afraid to express themselves, go on adventures, take risks, and most importantly, play to your heart's content. Search for the part of you that enjoys life as it comes with all its ups and downs. Teach your inner child that obstacles or pitfalls don't compromise your safety but that they teach you to pick yourself up.

11. Get Rid of Your Sexual Guilt and Shame

In most cases, one's inner child suffers from severe sexual guilt and shame. These negative emotions are usually a product of family repression, bullying or ridicule, enmeshment, incest, and other traumas. Few people realize that our upbringing can greatly influence our sexuality as adults. These wounds can appear as sexual anorexia or the rejection of all types of intimate relationships, sexual addictions, an addiction to pornography viewing, etc.

When a child has been subject to incest or enmeshment, they will end up repressing their sexuality in hopes of pushing away the parent who had hurt them. Not only that, but further into adulthood, the individual will struggle with feelings of guilt when it comes to sexual relationships. This may stand in the way of building healthy romantic relationships. To help your inner child overcome this shame, you need to reassure them that it's not wrong to be curious about sex. They need to understand that sexual urges and drives are normal and that they're nothing to be ashamed of. Finally, they are now safe, meaning that they don't need to hide their sexuality from the offending caregiver anymore.

Quiz: Which Inner Child Healing Benefits Have I Experienced?

Use this quiz as a guide to help you measure your progress throughout the inner child healing journey.

- My overall quality of life has improved.
- I no longer suffer from mental cloudiness.
- My anxiety is not as severe as it used to be.
- I am experiencing fewer or diminished symptoms of depression.
- My vitality has improved.
- My sense of curiosity and wonder is now revived.
- I believe I can stand up for myself better.
- I have a clearer understanding of my boundaries, and I make sure that no one oversteps them.
- I can say "no" whenever I need to.
- I can cultivate better intrapersonal relationships.
- I am more emotionally mature and can control my feelings better.

- I am more "myself" than I was before.
- I am no longer ashamed of my past painful experiences.
- I don't feel guilty about my unhealthy coping mechanisms. I realize that, at one point, it was the only way I could've survived.
- I am not worried about what people think of me. I don't allow anyone's opinions to dictate my mental state.
- I don't feel resentful toward my family and the people who hurt me.
- I don't feel shameful when it comes to my sexuality.
- I can identify narcissistic behaviors and unhealthy patterns.
- I speak my mind and no longer repress my thoughts and feelings for fear of hurting someone.

You may not have really understood how relevant your inner child was until you decided to give this book a read. You were never aware of how big of a role your younger self plays in how you think, act, react, and feel today. However, once you start taking steps toward inner child work, you'd feel like you opened yourself up to a new world that you never knew existed. Inner child work is all about realizing that many of the emotions that we experience as adults, such as fear and insecurity, are brought over by the inner child. Today, you are grown and different from how you used to be. Because your younger self was never granted the right to have opinions, you grew up keeping them to yourself, denying yourself the ability to be assertive. Once you see that this fear comes from the child within, you can calm and soothe them. Being compassionate and understanding can, over time, help you overcome the fears that weigh you down. You will gain clarity and self-awareness in your efforts to heal your inner child.

Chapter 10: Healing Your Inner Child Challenge

Our emotions and overall happiness highly depend on our childhood experiences. Many people don't understand that they have to account for their childhood when planning for the future. We are spiritually connected with several versions of ourselves, which we must remember when deciding which way to go. This doesn't mean that you should stay stuck in the past or let previous negative events hold you back. We mean that you need to determine how your past influences your current life. Pinpointing unhelpful patterns, problematic behaviors, and detrimental coping mechanisms is the only way you'll get one step closer to leading a happier life. You need to explore how you were raised, find out how you make your choices, and evaluate the quality of your connections throughout the course of your life. If you don't take the time to figure out the state of your mental, emotional, social, and spiritual health, you'll never be able to tell what you need to do to change your life for the better and get rid of the things that hold you back from achieving the things you deserve.

Your inner child is a more critical part of your mind, joy, freedom, playfulness, friendliness, and compassion than you realize. This part of yourself represents the aspect of you that desires to feel loved, safe, comfortable, and protected. The reason why it's so relevant to your spiritual health is that it is a combination of your fundamental and innate emotions, imagination, creativity, and vulnerability that you repressed as you grew older. The inner child is, you guessed it, the childlike aspect of your being. It is the part of you that reacts impulsively or lashes out whenever things don't go how they want. It is basically everything you've learned and experienced during your developmental stages of life. The younger child inside is your essence. It is the intrinsically innocent, playful, and uncomplicated part of your consciousness.

Now that you understand that the concept of healing the inner child is an important step towards spiritual well-being and awakening, you are now prepared to go on about this process in the form of a challenge. This chapter serves as a 30-day guide to healing your inner child, ultimately allowing you to reach spiritual awakening.

Day 1: Identify Your Inner Child Archetype

- Do the "What Inner Child Archetype Am I?" Quiz. Complete the quiz in chapter 2 to determine your inner child's archetype.
- Detach. When identifying your inner child archetype, you need to be very mindful when it comes to what you're feeling and thinking. You need to be sure that you're exploring the beliefs and values that belong to you, not those imposed on you by your community or society. Detach yourself from the world around you and have a deep conversation with your inner child. Find out how they feel, what they're thinking about, what they need, which activities make them happy, etc.
- Practice Self-Compassion. Many people have the wrong idea about practicing self-compassion. The process isn't all about hyping yourself up or telling yourself that there's nothing to feel bad about. On the contrary, feeling bad is fine, just like feeling happy is okay. Self-compassion is all about developing mindfulness toward your childhood experiences and acknowledging the child within. This means that the last thing you should do is to play down your insecurities, sadness, or fears. Make sure you are present and let your inner child know they are wanted, loved, and valid.

Day 2: Practice Awareness of Your Inner Child

- Go for a long walk in nature. Taking a long walk in nature can help you feel grounded and in tune with your surroundings. It can also give you mental clarity and help you acknowledge your

thoughts and emotions. Be fully present in the moment and engage all your senses.
- Practice Yoga. The Mountain is a very easy yoga pose that anyone can do. If you're more experienced with yoga, you can do any other pose you like as long as it makes you feel comfortable and focused. The Mountain pose can help you with your posture, body awareness, and alignment.
- Plant both feet flat on the floor as you stand up straight. Your heels should be parted as your big toes touch. Roll your shoulder blades down while lifting your chest. Move your chin inward as you elongate your head. Place your arms by your sides with your palms facing forward. Your throat should be constricted while you breathe through your nose. Maintain the pose for 5 to 10 breaths.
- Meditate. Meditate for 5 minutes before you go to bed.

Day 3: Journal about Your Inner Child

- Write a letter to your inner child. Write a letter to your younger self from the point of view of a loving, supportive parent. Explain how you will protect them and express how much you're proud of them. Tell them that you love them and are working on giving them the life and happiness they deserve. You can even apologize if you want to. Write from your heart.
- Write about your needs. Explore your younger self's sense of identity. Explore your most basic needs. What does your inner child long for? Is it love? Is it safe? Write about what your inner child needs to feel like themself.
- Come up with affirmations. Write affirmations expressing your value, unique traits, what you bring to the table, how you affect other people's lives, etc.

Day 4: Embrace the Hurt

- Meditate. Meditate for 5 minutes in the morning.
- Reflect. Retreat to a quiet and safe space. Detach from your environment and shift your full attention to your emotions. How do you feel right now? Think about your childhood and how your memories make you feel. Has anything changed since you decided to embark on your inner child healing journey? Does it

make you feel better or worse so far? Don't set your emotions aside, no matter how painful they may be. Acknowledge them and experience them fully.

Day 5: Engage Your Inner Child

- Spend time with children. Spend some time with kids and take part in activities they enjoy doing. If you have kids, give them a portion of your day. If you don't, you can offer to babysit your niece or a friend's child for the day. Don't be afraid to let your inner child come out.
- Let loose. Allow yourself to let loose today. If you're usually serious at work, it won't hurt to crack a joke or take things slow every once in a while. Be playful and have fun.
- Visualize. Visualize the future you want before you go to bed. Think about your future home, car, and job. How do you look? What does your style look like? Let your imagination run wild.

Day 5: Nurture Your Inner Child

- Have a conversation with your inner child. Acknowledge your inner child's presence and let them know that you wish to connect with them on a deeper level. Explain that their safety and comfort are your topmost priorities.
- Look at old photos. Look at old photos of yourself and say affirmations of protection, compassion, and love.
- Write about your decision to let go of old cycles. Write a letter to your inner child that includes everything they need to hear. This can be an apology letter that addresses the fact that they had to grow up so fast or that they were never nurtured the way they should've been.
- Give them a safe space to play. Think about the type of games you always wished you could play as a child, and make sure to do just that.

Day 6: Validate Their Emotions

- Release your emotions. Grab your journal and write down all your feelings and emotions. Be as expressive and detailed as possible, allowing nothing to remain unacknowledged or slip through the cracks.

- Meditate. Meditate for 5 minutes.
- Take a break. Take the day off from work and responsibilities. Take it easy and go with the flow.
- Burn incense. Burning incense can serve as a great mood booster. It can also relieve stress and anxiety.
- Do something fun. Do anything you typically enjoy doing, whether it's practicing a hobby, going out with friends, or watching a movie.

Day 7: Re-Examine Our Boundaries

- Say no. Think before doing any favors or following others. Think about whether this is something you really want to do. Don't be afraid to turn down requests or invitations you're not up for.
- Reflect on your relationships. Think about all the relationships in your life. What are your familial, social, professional, and romantic relationships like? What does your definition of a healthy relationship look like? Do any of your relationships in life match that description? Do you feel uncomfortable when hanging around some people? Why is that? Would you describe any of your relationships as unhealthy? Why? What do you plan on doing about it?
- What are your boundaries? What are your boundaries when it comes to the way you interact with others? Are they different from your boundaries back then? Do you allow people to overstep your boundaries? If so, why do you do it, and how does it make you feel?

Day 8: Ground Yourself

- Take a long walk in nature and make sure you're present and connected with your surroundings.
- Practice yoga. You can do some light poses like The Mountain pose or Warrior I. If you're up for a challenge, watch a beginner's yoga video on YouTube and follow along.
- Burn sage.
- Practice deep breathing. Breathe deeply for 2 to 3 minutes.

Day 9: Get Moving

- Stretch. Do light stretches for 5 to 10 minutes.
- Exercise. Do your favorite form of exercise for 30 minutes.
- Go for the stairs. Take the elevator instead of the stairs. If you have a quick errand to run, walk or bike those few blocks instead of driving or taking a cab. Release your energy.

Day 10: Heal by Helping Others – Lend someone a hand. Does a friend look like they have been struggling lately? Ask what you can do for them and try to help them out. Working on qualities like kindness and compassion is crucial when doing inner child work.

- Pet an animal or play with a baby.
- Smile at strangers.
- Do a random act of kindness.

Day 11: Take Control

- Come up with a to-do list. Write a to-do list of everything you need to do throughout the day. Prioritize the tasks from most to least important. If you have nothing to do today, it's time to work on any tasks you've been putting off.
- Declutter your home. Come up with a fun way to declutter your home. Not only will this instill a sense of accomplishment, but it will remind your inner child that responsibilities don't have to be burdensome.
- Detach. Let go of unhelpful thoughts and emotions.

Day 12: Manage Your Emotions

- Notice your feelings. Check in on your emotions multiple times throughout the day. Carry a mood journal around where you can write all about your emotions and the reactions they trigger.
- Meditate. Retreat to a safe space and meditate for 3 to 5 minutes whenever you need to.

- Practice deep breathing. Breathe deeply for 3 minutes several times during the day.
- Think before you react. Take a moment to think about whether it's the appropriate time and place to express your emotions.

Day 13: Practice Mindfulness

- Tune into your senses. Stop every once in a while to engage all your senses in your experiences. For instance, when you're eating, feel the texture of the food or how the spoon feels against your fingertips, savor the food with your eyes, enjoy its taste, take in its smell, and listen to the surrounding environment.
- Practice self-compassion. Treat yourself the way you would treat a friend.
- Shift your attention. Sit down for a minute whenever you're having negative thoughts and shift your attention to your breathing.

Day 14: Grow Your Self-Awareness

- Be objective. Think about yourself objectively. What are your accomplishments? Did the things that made you happy as a child still make you happy now?
- Think about your goals. What are your goals and plans for the future?
- Meditate. Meditate for 10 minutes before bed.

Day 15: Acknowledge Your Progress

- Practice deep breathing. Breathe deeply for 2 to 3 minutes.
- Stretch. Stretch lightly for 5 minutes.
- Journal. Write about your progress and what you've accomplished throughout this journey so far. How have the past 15 days changed you? What do you expect to achieve by the end of the challenge?
- Exercise. Do your favorite form of exercise for 15 minutes.
- Reward yourself. Reward your inner child for making it this far and do something that makes them happy.

Day 16: Release the Past

- Do an emotional release. Write down everything you're feeling and thinking about.
- Identify your emotional loop. Are there certain emotions that you experience every day? What triggers them? What can you do to counter them?
- Replace negative emotions with positive ones. Did you know that you can train yourself to feel positive emotions in situations that typically make you feel resentful or sad? If something doesn't turn out the way you hoped it would, you will undoubtedly feel bad. However, you can alleviate those negative emotions and even eventually turn them into positive ones by reshaping your thought process. Instead of viewing this as a failure, you can think of it as a learning experience.

Day 17: Grow Your Trust

- Stop comparing. Stop comparing yourself to others.
- Don't worry about the opinions of others.
- Restructure your "What Ifs." Turn negative what-ifs like "what if I fail" into positive ones like "what if it works out for the best?"

Day 18: Connect with Your Inner Child

Dedicate this day to connecting with your inner child. Listen to everything they have to say and feel. Take the day off from work if you need to. Engage in activities that made you the happiest in your childhood. Explore your childhood wounds, where they came from, what feelings they're associated with, and what events trigger these feelings. Reassure your inner child that they're now safe and protected.

Day 19: Go Offline

- Exercise. Practice your favorite form of exercise for 15 minutes.
- Go offline. Take a break from electronics for the day.
- Go out for ice cream. Treat yourself to ice cream or stop by your favorite drive-through from your childhood on your way home.
- Get creative. Draw, paint, dance, or practice any other creative activity of your choice.
- Practice one of your hobbies.

Day 20: Forgive

Day 20 is all about forgiveness. Forgive someone who hurt you in your childhood. Think about what they did and how it made you feel. Imagine these thoughts and emotions floating away and out of your mind. Forgive them for your own peace of mind. If you're not on talking terms with that person, you don't need to reach out to them if you don't wish to. Remember, you're forgiving them for your own good.

Day 21: Put Yourself First

- Meditate. Meditate for 5 minutes.
- Do something that makes your inner child happy.
- Say no. Say no to the things you don't want to do.
- Practice self-care. Take a long bath, a nap, visit a spa, or practice any other form of self-care.

Day 22: Fill the Gaps

What are some consequences you fell victim to in your childhood? Realize that these are things you can rise up against now that you're an adult. For instance, if you didn't receive adequate care as a child, you can take steps to ensure that you're always prioritized and cared for. If you grew up in poverty, you could come up with a financial plan, learn how to budget and save, and take steps to increase your income.

Day 23: Go on an Adventure

Whether you decide to go to the fair or pack your bags and leave the city for the day, you should do something spontaneous. Embrace your innate desire for adventure and allow your inner child inside to flourish. Bonus points if you manage to do something you've always wanted to do as a child!

Day 24: Stand Up for Yourself

- Practice self-love. Think about 4 qualities you like about your past and current self.
- Stand your ground. Don't be afraid to express your opinions even when others don't agree with them.

- Stand up for yourself. Defend yourself whenever someone disrespects you or looks down on you. Don't allow anyone to insult you.

Day 25: Write a Letter

Write a letter to the people who left the most significant impact on you throughout your life. Focus primarily on your childhood. Write down how they made you feel and how they changed you for better or worse. Are there certain events that you associate with those people? What memories and emotions do those events trigger? What would you say to those people if you could speak up with no consequences? Once you're done, read it out loud and imagine that you're talking to those people. Once you're ready to let go, burn that letter.

Day 26: Manage Your Anger

- Exercise. Practice your favorite form of exercise for 15 minutes.
- Practice yoga. You can do some light poses like the mountain pose and Warrior I.
- Practice deep breathing. Breathe deeply for 2 to 3 minutes.
- Take a time-out. Whenever you feel anger building up inside of you, practice mindfulness.

Day 27: Overcome Your Sadness

- Practice transforming your thoughts into positive ones.
- Reach out to loved ones. You may be struggling with feelings of loneliness and an inclination to self-isolate. Make sure to reach out to people who can help you get past this difficult time.
- Care for your inner child. Don't forget to tend to your inner child's needs.

Day 28: Fight the Remorse

- Explore the source of guilt.
- Explain that there's nothing you could've done differently.
- Work on replacing your unhelpful habits with positive ones.
- Consider therapy.

Day 29: Face Your Fears

- Meditate. Meditate for 10 minutes.
- Be an optimist. Expect great things to happen throughout the day.
- Overcome a fear. Take steps toward overcoming a fear.
- Get outside of your comfort zone. Do something you've always wanted to do but couldn't because you doubted your abilities.
- Take chances.

Day 30: Embrace the Healing

Reflect on your inner child's healing journey. How did the past 30 days make you feel? Do you feel like you've changed in any way? Which of the activities mentioned in the challenge are you willing to incorporate into your lifestyle? Which ones are you planning on leaving behind? What steps will you take to maintain your progress?

Conclusion

As you have learned from this book, your inner child represents the culmination of negative emotions hidden in the depths of your soul. By making the child within you happier, you are transforming your soul. Whether this transformation means healing a wounded soul from past trauma, spiritual awakening, or rising to a higher state of spiritual awareness - it's entirely up to you. However, before you start connecting with your inner child, you must understand how it's shaped and how it impacts your life as an adult. You will also have to explore the exact archetype of your inner child - as this can determine your approach to improving your spiritual well-being. Each type has different strengths and weaknesses, so finding out which one lives within you can help you avoid mistakes when trying to form a connection.

Once you know your inner child's archetype, you can move on to learn more about the child's relation to your wounded soul. Understanding your wounded soul is only one of the numerous benefits of discovering your inner child, but it also comes with many challenges. Beyond discovering, exploring your wounded soul also encompasses accepting your inner child with all its positives and negatives. Because while one's inner child has an inherently cheery disposition, traumatic experiences can turn this into a rather somber tone.

Accepting your inner channel means that you've become open to communicating with them and are ready to discover all the ways you can get in touch with your soul. One of the most recommended techniques is meditation. Love-based mindful meditation techniques are particularly known to promote a higher level of spiritual awareness by calming your body and mind and replacing your negative thought processes with loving ones. Journaling is another practice with a positive impact on healing wounded souls. Recording your thoughts and emotions can uncover patterns that indicate a spiritual imbalance.

Of course, there are many other ways to raise your inner child awareness - with many of them pointing towards the best healing paths for your wounded soul. Most of these techniques operate on the same mindfulness principle as meditative exercises do. By simply shifting the attention from your body and mind, they can make you more aware of your soul's needs. That being said, if you're not versed in spirituality, learning most of these techniques will definitely represent some challenges. Fortunately, this book will prepare you for all the possible obstacles you can face during this process by advising you on how to work through them and learn from them when striving for spiritual growth. By overcoming these challenges, you will become much stronger. You will learn how to harvest all the benefits that healing your wounded soul can provide and how to multiply these spiritual gifts.

Last but not least, you will be introduced to the concept of viewing the healing of your inner child as a challenge. Not only is healing the inner child a crucial step towards ensuring spiritual well-being, but by making it into a challenge, you are encouraging yourself to do your best. You can use any of the techniques mentioned in this book or any other mindfulness exercise you can tailor to your needs.

Here's another book by Mari Silva that you might like

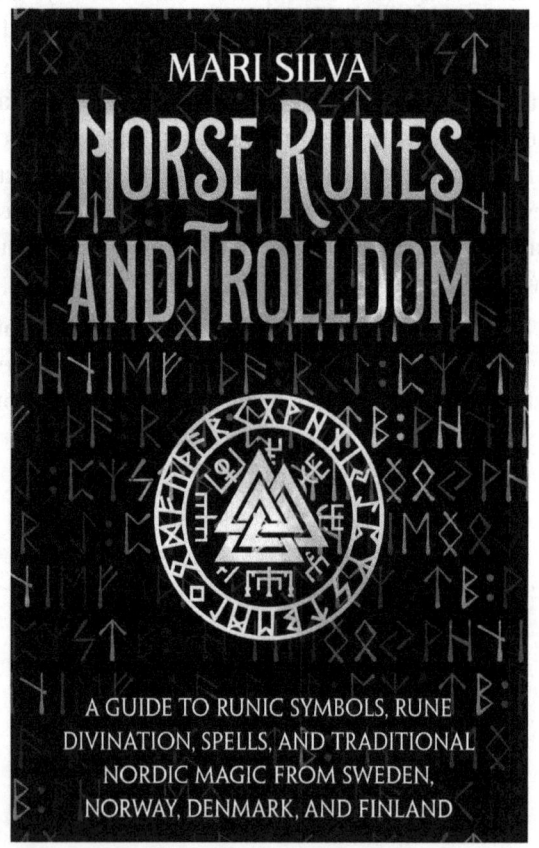

Your Free Gift
(only available for a limited time)

Thanks for getting this book! If you want to learn more about various spirituality topics, then join Mari Silva's community and get a free guided meditation MP3 for awakening your third eye. This guided meditation mp3 is designed to open and strengthen ones third eye so you can experience a higher state of consciousness. Simply visit the link below the image to get started.

https://spiritualityspot.com/meditation

References

Casement, A. (2006). The shadow. The handbook of Jungian psychology: Theory, practice, and applications.

Chappell, S., Cooper, E., & Trippe, G. (2019). Shadow work for leadership development. Journal of Management Development.

Dourley, J. P. (1994). IN THE SHADOW OF THE MONOTHEISMS: JUNG'S. Jung and the monotheisms: Judaism, Christianity, and Islam.

Grosso, C. (2015). Everything Mind: What I've Learned About Hard Knocks, Spiritual Awakening, and the Mind-blowing Truth of it All. Sounds True.

Gilmore, J. (2019). Community Art as Shadow Work. Jung Journal.

Karpiak, I. E. (2003). The shadow: mining its dark treasury for teaching and adult development. Canadian Journal of University Continuing Education.

Kremer, J. W., & Rothberg, D. (1999). Facing the collective shadow. ReVision.

McLaughlin, R. G. (2014). Shadow work in support of the adult developmental journey. Lesley University.

Mayer, C. H. (2017). Shame—"A soul-feeding emotion": Archetypal work and the transformation of the shadow of shame in a group development process. In The Value of Shame. Springer, Cham.

Morley, C. (2021). Dreaming Through Darkness: Shine Light into the Shadow to Live the Life of Your Dreams. Hay House, Inc.

Onyett, S., & Hill, M. (2012). Integrating Shadow Work and Appreciative Inquiry Reflections on Structural Inequalities, Polarities and Hurt. AI Practitioner.

Sol, M., & Luna, A. (2019). The spiritual awakening process. Luna & Sol Pty Ltd.

Stokke, C., & Rodriguez, M. C. Spiritual Awakening Experiences: A Phenomenological Study in Transpersonal Psychology.

Sutton, N. (2021). Consciousness rising guiding you through spiritual awakening and beyond. Hay House, Inc.

Wilber, K., Patten, T., Leonard, A., & Morelli, M. (2008). Integral life practice: A 21st-century blueprint for physical health, emotional balance, mental clarity, and spiritual awakening. Shambhala Publications.

Zweig, C., & Wolf, S. (1997). Romancing the shadow: Illuminating the dark side of the soul. Ballantine Books

What is your inner child (and why it's important you get to know them)? (2021, March 26). My Online Therapy. https://myonlinetherapy.com/what-is-your-inner-child-and-why-its-important-you-get-to-know-them/

Davis, S. (n.d.). The wounded inner child. Cptsdfoundation.Org. https://cptsdfoundation.org/2020/07/13/the-wounded-inner-child/

Goldstein, E. (2021, April 6). What is an Inner Child? Integrative Psychotherapy & Trauma Treatment. https://integrativepsych.co/new-blog/what-is-an-inner-child

How to know if you have a wounded inner child (and how to heal). (2021, March 2). The Mighty. https://themighty.com/2021/03/trauma-wounded-inner-child-how-to-know-heal/

Jacobson, S. (2017, March 23). What is the "inner child"? Harley TherapyTM Blog. https://www.harleytherapy.co.uk/counselling/what-is-the-inner-child.htm

Kahn, J. (2019, November 15). Why healing your Inner Child is important. G&STC. https://www.gstherapycenter.com/blog/2019/11/15/why-healing-your-inner-child-is-important

Luna, A. (2019, April 6). 25 signs you have a wounded inner child (and how to heal). LonerWolf. https://lonerwolf.com/feeling-safe-inner-child/

What is inner child work? A guide to healing your inner child. (2020, December 31). Mindbodygreen. https://www.mindbodygreen.com/articles/inner-child-work/

What is your inner child (and why it's important you get to know them). (2021, March 26). My Online Therapy. https://myonlinetherapy.com/what-is-your-inner-child-and-why-its-important-you-get-to-know-them/

The importance of embracing your inner child. (n.d.). Beliefnet.Com. https://www.beliefnet.com/inspiration/articles/the-importance-of-embracing-your-inner-child.aspx

Aquarian. (2019, January 27). Deep dive into the nature child, a primal archetype. Enlighten Up! With The Aquarian. http://www.aquarianonline.com/deep-dive-into-the-nature-child-a-primal-archetype/

Banday, N. (2020, May 4). What is The Child Archetype? - Take a journey into the human psyche. Learn how we operate on a basic level. - Take a journey into the human psyche. Learn how we operate on a basic level. Navigation for Daily Living.

ChelseaC. (2018, November 9). Find out which of the 6 Child archetypes you fit, and start embracing it. The Odyssey Online. https://www.theodysseyonline.com/whats-my-child-archetype

Couch, S. (2015, August 28). Healing the inner child archetype. Wild Gratitude. https://www.wildgratitude.com/healing-the-inner-child-archetype/

knowyourarchetypes. (2020a, June 23). Child archetype. Know Your Archetypes. https://knowyourarchetypes.com/child-archetype/

knowyourarchetypes. (2020b, August 19). Divine Child Archetype. Know Your Archetypes. https://knowyourarchetypes.com/divine-child-archetype/

knowyourarchetypes. (2020c, August 19). Wounded Child Archetype. Know Your Archetypes. https://knowyourarchetypes.com/wounded-child-archetype/

The child archetype. (2020, February 4). Make A Dent Leadership. https://www.makeadentleadership.com/the-child-archetype/

The "eternal child" function of your personality type - Mystical Analytics. (2021, January 3). Mystical Analytics -. https://mysticalanalytics.com/the-eternal-child-function-of-your-personality-type/

Which Inner Child Archetype are You? (2017, May 23). Jennifer Soldner.

(N.d.). Fcusd.Org. https://www.fcusd.org/cms/lib03/CA01001934/Centricity/Domain/1250/Archetype%20Survey.pdf

Davis, S. (n.d.). Discovering your inner child. Cptsdfoundation.Org. https://cptsdfoundation.org/2020/07/06/discovering-your-inner-child/

Discover your inner child. (2016, October 20). Exploring Your Mind. https://exploringyourmind.com/discover-inner-child/

Giovanis, N. (2021, January 6). Discovering your inner child. A Space Between. https://www.aspacebetween.com.sg/blog/discovering-your-inner-child

Inner child: 6 ways to find yours. (2020, June 26). Healthline. https://www.healthline.com/health/inner-child

Perkal, Z. (2015, April 2). How to find your inner child as an adult. Wanderlust. https://wanderlust.com/journal/find-inner-child/

Roxanne. (2017, April 26). 10 questions to uncover your inner child. TextMyJournal. https://www.textmyjournal.com/10-questions-uncover-inner-child/

Team Zoella. (2022, February 22). How to connect with your inner child to heal, evolve & blossom in adulthood. Zoella. https://zoella.co.uk/2022/02/22/how-to-connect-with-your-inner-child-to-heal-evolve-blossom-in-adulthood/

Neta, N. (2020, October 21). The journey of healing the inner child. Newport Institute. https://www.newportinstitute.com/resources/mental-health/inner-child/

8 tips for healing your inner child. (2021, September 9). Healthline. https://www.healthline.com/health/mental-health/inner-child-healing

Chen, L. (2015, October 19). 7 things your inner child needs to hear you say. Tiny Buddha. https://tinybuddha.com/blog/7-things-your-inner-child-needs-to-hear-you-say/

Coleman, K. (2022, February 23). Why you should embrace your inner child. Her Campus Media. https://www.hercampus.com/school/illinois-state/why-you-should-embrace-your-inner-child/

Embrace Your Inner Child: 5 Ways to embrace your inner child today! (2017, September 8). Girlandtonic.Co.Uk; lauriemcallister. https://girlandtonic.co.uk/embrace-your-inner-child/

Embracing your inner child. (2017, September 14). Nature Explore. https://natureexplore.org/embracing-your-inner-child-2/

Fuller, J. (2018, July 30). Embrace your inner child –. Jane Fuller. https://www.janefuller.co.uk/blog/2018/7/30/embrace-your-inner-child

Meyerowitz, A. (2020, November 20). Why we should embrace our inner child and 5 ways to do it. Red Online. https://www.redonline.co.uk/health-self/self/a34725323/how-to-embrace-inner-child/

www.ingramcontent.com/pod-product-compliance
Lightning Source LLC
Chambersburg PA
CBHW072155200426
43209CB00052B/1262